Tears of an Orphan Heart

Heal the father wound & embrace God as Abba

TE'AIRE GRIFFIN

Tears of an Orphan Heart

Heal the father wound & embrace God as Abba

TE'AIRE GRIFFIN

Printed in the United States of America by
T&J Publishers (Atlanta, GA.)
www.TandJPublishers.com

Cover Design by Kenish Magwood
Book Format/Layout by Timothy Flemming, Jr.

ISBN: 978-1-7345105-1-5

To contact author, go to:

www.TeaireGriffin.com
Facebook: Te'Aire Griffin
Instagram: TeAire Griffin
Youtube: TeAire Griffin

DEDICATIONS

This book is dedicated to the fathers in my life, my biological father, stepfather, and spiritual fathers. Thank you for leaving such an impression on my life.

This book is also dedicated to my mother, Sharron Griffin. Thank you for your love, and your example of strength, courage, and determination. Thank you for carrying me, raising me, and stopping at nothing to give me the best life possible.

"And you did not receive the 'spirit of religious
duty,' leading you back into the fear of never being
good enough. But you have receive the 'Spirit of
full acceptance,' enfolding you in the family of God.
And you will never feel orphaned, for as he rises up
within us, our spirits join him in saying the words of
tender affection, 'Beloved Father!' For the Holy
Spirit makes God's fatherhood real to us as he
whispers into our innermost being, 'You are
God's beloved child!'"
- (Romans 8:15-16, The Passion Translation)

TABLE OF CONTENTS

Chapter 1

WHERE'S MY DADDY?

"I DO NOT HAVE ONE - MY MOTHER IS MY FATHER." That was my response to my tenth-grade history teacher during a discussion we were having during the second-period class. That day, I was sitting in the back of the classroom with all of the cool kids. I sat next to the diamond -shaped window door where the sunlight would shine through on me. The teacher asked all of the students about the whereabouts of their fathers. I boldly yelled my answer from the back of the room. I was being blunt and speaking what I believed. The look on everyone's faces, particularly those who grew up with their fathers, appeared puzzled at first. The room got so quiet you could hear a pen drop. At that moment, it was as if everyone's eyes had fallen on me; this made me feel obligated to offer an explanation for my comment.

I was resentful towards my father because my mother was the only father I knew. She was the one I saw every day. She provided my clothes, shoes, and kept a hot meal on the dinner table each night. She would drive me to school each morning and wait in that long car-rider line to pick me up from school each afternoon. She purchased the house we lived in, providing me with a roof and bed. My mother worked every day; she took no days off. She worked as a hairdresser and a real estate agent, and she later pursued a Bachelor of Science degree in Nursing. She wanted to give us the best life a single mother could give us in the absence of the male parent. I don't know how she did it all; it's like she wore a huge "S" on her chest. My mother did what was needed to keep the lights on, water running, and a roof over our heads. To me, my mother had superpowers; she was strong, and she was always there for my siblings and me.

My mother raised four children on her own. She raised all of us to be God-fearing. Raising two boys and two girls, I never saw her crack under all of the pressure she was carrying. She did not break under the statistics, the abuse, nor hardships that come with life. My mother never missed a game of mine, a recital, meeting, birthday, or celebration for my siblings and me. My mother was a provider and a pro-tector, doing what a father was supposed to do. I watched a lot of television growing up, and the sitcoms would portray what a father was supposed to be. Unfortunately, that role was left open for my mother to fill. My mother had to put her dreams and goals on hold to see about her children. Her children were her priority. My mother had to put many of her dreams on hold to strive at being my only present par-ent. She'd talk all of the time about becoming an anesthesi-ologist. Still, she gave that dream up for my siblings and me and never complained.

My mother had to play both parents; she had to have twice the strength, twice the availability, and twice the love. Although I did not fully understand what she was facing, my mother did the best she could. It was like I got a two-for-one-special. I got everything I needed in one person. My mother carried the weight of two responsibilities. She bore more than she was designed by God to endure, and she did not break. She realized that if my father wasn't going to do his part, someone had to do it—so she stepped up.

Growing up, my mother was the oldest of four girls. My grandfather had no sons. He taught his girls to never wait for a man to do anything for them. He taught them how to be independent.

My mother took on the role of a father better than most men. She was the disciplinarian—and she did not spare the rod. (Thank you, mom.) She provided our family with direction like a compass. She protected our home like a guard dog. Absolutely nothing got past her, and if she caught you, it was off with your head. My mother fought for me when I was right, and even when I was wrong. She'd address my wrongs later on, though. She was my Superwoman, my everything. She was my mother.

Interestingly, close by lived the one person who could fill the void in my heart and relieve my mother of the responsibility of playing dad. My father lived just five miles down the road from us. I'd spend hours looking out the window, waiting for my dad to show up, knowing he was right around the corner; still, I had little interaction with him. It is one thing when your father is far away from you, out of reach, or you've never seen him before. Still, it's another thing when your father lives in a neighborhood just down the street from you, and you have to pass his house daily. To be estranged from a father that close can leave you feeling even more unwanted and rejected.

So, when it comes to Father's Day, whom should I celebrate:

A) Someone who gave me life one day
B) Someone present in my life every day

Most people would go with option B.

How could I celebrate a man I had no relationship with, a man who gave me life and that's all? Giving me life didn't make him a father; that just made him a sperm donor. To me, my mother deserved to be celebrated during Father's Day. She did more for me than any father I had known; on top of that, she did what no other father did: she stayed. I would hear other kids talk about their dads; their dads sounded like my mother. So I'd wonder if we were celebrating the man or his role? The man? No, thank you. To celebrate the role well, for father's day, the award for greatest role of father goes to my mother. All day, everyday.

Back to the class discussion. That day in class, while discussing fathers, I responded, "You mean, my sperm donor, right?" The entire class went crazy with laughter, but I was not trying to be funny; I was speaking from my heart. My heart was wounded and in desperate need of healing. At first, however, I thought I was perfectly fine—I was more like a broken chair that appeared stable after being repaired with duct tape and gorilla glue. But like that fractured chair, I could function to a certain degree, as long as nothing too heavy weighed on my shoulders. From a distance, I looked fine, but up close, you could see where I'd been patched up by someone who didn't have the proper skills to fix me nor the wisdom to take me to the shop for repairs. For a moment, picture standing before a big, beautiful house. The house's exterior is well-kept. The house's interior, however, is in bad shape; it's dirty, there's writing all over the walls, everything is broken, and every room is cluttered with junk. That was how I was. This might be how you are too. From the outside, everyone looks beautiful, but you can never know a person's actual condition until you spend time getting to know them within.

DYSFUNCTIONAL BUT STILL FUNCTIONING

I didn't want to hear anyone tell me what was wrong with me. Looking back, I was a walking, talking wound; I was open to the air and infectious to everyone I came in contact with. I made light of my father's absence. I trivialized an epidemic in my community. I wanted to be close to my father but was too prideful to admit it. I did not know any better. Fatherlessness was normal where I came from, and if they were not absent, they were blue-moon-dads (you'd see them every now and then when they dropped off money or toys). Most of these "sperm donors" were married to the streets or too busy taking care of other women and their children. When my father left us, he went to play daddy in another woman's house. He was absent for us but fully present for them, being a step-dad. He stepped up for the other woman's children. Still, no matter what home these sperm donors were in, they were clueless concerning raising children. They'd often overcompensate with things like money and gifts and then disappear for months at a time. From a distance, they'd send child-support payments to help pay the bills. They didn't know how to raise daughters—how to love them and paint a picture of what a man should be so that she'd have excellent standards when it came to choosing a partner.

At the time, I was 15-years-old. I had not spoken to the man who gave me life in months. For me, it was out of sight, out of mind. As long as I did not see my father, he did not run across my mind. This is how I remained functional. Just thinking about the fact that he was so distant emotionally, and yet, so close physically made the pain of feeling unwanted more intense. I would feel like that broken chair carrying a weight too heavy to bear. I didn't want to get a headache thinking about the whole situation. I chose instead to pretend he didn't even exist so that I could make my life easier.

I stopped being the little girl staring out the window, wondering where my dad was. He made too many empty promises to me, claiming he would pick me up only to never come. I was no longer waiting for him to pull up in the driveway so I could rush out of the door to greet him, bouncing up and down as we made our way to the front door. I'd picture the entire scenario in my mind, how hearing his footsteps as he approached the door would cause me to be overwhelmed with eagerness and excitement. Before he would even get to knock on the door, I'd swing the doors open, jump into his arms, wrap my arms around his neck, and rest my head on his chest. This would be the perfect image of God's perfect love, of how God designed for fathers and their daughters to embrace. I'd imagine him saying to me, "I miss you, baby-girl." I always wanted this kind of love from a father, but not just me. I believe all children long for the love of their fathers. We are all born with the innate desire to be loved and have companionship. In Genesis 2:18, the Lord God said, "It is not good for man to be alone." I wanted my father's love, but I didn't know how to put it in words. I decided to bury my desire as if burying a coffin during a funeral. As far as I was concerned, my father was dead to me.

As I got older, I filled the void in my heart that my father's absence left with other things that were not good for me. My soul had a sweet tooth and craved the type of candy that left cavities and holes in my life. I developed a sweet tooth for bad relationships that left me devastated from the inside out. I craved love, praise, affirmation, and attention from the wrong men. I longed to hear someone tell me I was good enough. My aunts, grandmother, great grandmother, and mom, after doing for me all they could, couldn't erase the fact that my dad's absence was deeply affecting me. This was a big deal to me, even if I pretended it wasn't. My family did everything they could to fill the hole in my heart, but I needed a root canal, and the fill-in they gave me was temporary. The source of my internal pain was still there, lying beneath the surface, ready for another shock-wave.

My dad's absence had become normal, his broken promises a routine. My heart began to feel numb. Is it supposed to be like this? Must the majority of African American children grow up without a father? Or must they have strained relationships with their fathers? The pain of these young people becomes obvious whenever they're asked about these blue-moon-fathers. Their responses usually sound like this: "I don't need that n*$#@! I am good without him!" That sentiment was carried by many of my fellow peers who agreed with me that day in class. We had come to accept the fact that our fathers were not in our lives, and we all decided that it made no difference.

We did not have group discussions or press conferences about our absence fathers. There was no time for lying under the night's starry skies and imagining our fathers being in our lives. It seemed like fathers were not necessary since life went on without them. We had everything we needed without them. Without my dad around, I still had everything I needed. I had a roof over my head, food on the table, clothes on my back, Christmas, family functions, and celebrations without him. I made educational strides without him and his influence, graduating from High School with my diploma and obtaining my Bachelor's in Business Administration with a concentration in Accounting. I walked across both stages of educational advancement without him. I accomplished a lot of things without my father, too many to name. I was numb internally, though, because of the pain of not having my father in my life. I began to feel as if good fathers didn't exist, at least not within my community. These men were good enough to create babies, but not good enough to raise them. They'd disappear and casts shadows every now and then on their children's lives.

My father was not wholly absent; he was more like an eclipse—they come around rarely and are always a sight to see. I was two-years-old when my mother and father went their separate ways, and the consistency of my father's presence decreased dramatically. Now that all three of us were no longer under the same roof, the initial feeling that he would always be in my life rang through my mind; he even made such a claim loudly in the atmosphere. But after breaking his promise to come and see me a couple of times, it got more comfortable for him to continue this trend. I am not sure what happened, but from my perspective, my dad failed to consider my feelings, emotions, and need for his presence. These eclipses also happened when I heard things about my father.

Let's go back in time a little further. Let's visit the day Pandora's box flipped open. I'll never forget that night. I was lying at the foot of my aunt's bed, kicking my feet up and down and saying to my aunt, "I am my father's only child." I could see my aunt's expression clearly. It was as if she knew something I did not. She corrected me and said, "You have other siblings." I was floored. I felt confused. This did not make any sense. I thought to myself, "There are more of us?" The thought of this placed more pressure on me.

I did not believe her at all. To prove her point, my aunt called my father's sister, who confirmed that I was not the only child. My little world was crushed. The idea of a decent man was fading. My father's sister said, "It is true. You have other sisters." Not one sister, but several sisters. The last little bit of faith I had for my father to step up and be a better man washed down the drain. I felt crushed over the fact that I could walk right past my siblings on the streets and not even know they're my sisters. It's crazy because that's what happened. My family and I joined an amazing church around the corner from my grandmother's home. I made friends very quickly with a young lady I'd just met while there. Because I'm naturally social, I didn't think anything of the fact that we connected so quickly. It was not strange at all. I just loved this young girl. Then one day, after church, my father came over for a visit. He told me that the young girl I'd become acqauinted with at church was my sister. "My sister?" I thought. "You mean sisters in the Lord," I responded laughingly.

"No," he exclaimed. "Ciara (the young girl's name) is my daughter." The cat was out of the bag. I'd just discovered that the young lady I'd become friends with was my sister. Neither one of us had any idea that we were related.

What was I supposed to do with this information? I was just starting middle school. I was excited for my sister, but I was still emotionally distraught. No one knew what I was experiencing. I was angry, happy, disappointed, excited, confused, and frustrated at the same time. But I was trying to bury my emotions like a dog burying a bone in the back-yard. I was so angry with my dad for not being honest with me, feeling as if a real father would never keep such secrets from his own children. I felt abandoned and betrayed by him. At that point, I began to tell myself he was dead to me. I so desired to turn my heart to stone so that I could feel nothing for him. I didn't want him in my life anymore. Of course, I'd eventually have to undergo a healing in my heart before I could reach my full potential as a person. But these are a few of my earliest memories of my dad. They weaved themselves into my personality and helped to shape how I perceived life.

Chapter 2

THE IDENTITY, NECESSITY, AND ROLE OF A FATHER

THERE ARE SEVERAL ADJECTIVES THAT ARE USED TO describe a father are. They are:

- Protector
- Provider
- Prophet
- Priest
- One who affirms
- Leader
- Authority Figure
- Friend
- Example

When a father is missing, identity is not given; discipline is not given, and you even lack a sense of safety and security.

In the Bible, God is known as our Father. I'd hear this a lot. And when people would tell me this, I'd respond, "You mean the silent man upstairs that allowed my father to be the way he was towards me?" There was no way I was letting another "father" get close to me. Other men tried to be father figures, yet, to my surprise, they were unsuccessful because they left too. How hard is it to be a father if you are not with the mother? There was no consistent male presence in my life. When they were ready to go, they did just that. Those men taught me that when they were finished with someone or something, they had no qualms with walking away. They could do this with no strings attached and no remorse. So every belief that I had about a father had been perverted by negative experiences. Even when it came to God the Father, I figured He was like the so-called fathers I'd known growing up. I was okay with referring to God as anything but the Heavenly Father.

The question "Where's my daddy?" turned into "Where is God?" What did he have to say about all of this? Did he have an opinion? Or was he indifferent just like the many other father-figures in my life? I remember praying and asking God to visit me. I was making the sacrifice to pursue after Him, but I couldn't understand why He wasn't revealing Himself to me. Out of anger, I yelled at God, "You are just like my father! You told me if I draw nigh unto you, you would meet with me, and here I am coming, and you don't even show up. What kind of father is that?" I was broken, and I felt like God didn't want to be around me. I was already feeling rejected by my earthly father, and now my Heavenly Father also. I felt completely unloved and un-

22

wanted. I could barely bear my natural father's absence, but now I had to deal with a God who seemed absent in my life, and yet, people called Him omnipresent.

I always had a fear and reverence for God. Truthfully, I was terrified of Him. I believed that although God was invisible, He saw everything I did. When I pictured God in my mind, I always pictured Him as sitting in the sky looking down. That sense of distance didn't help to generate a sense of closeness to Him. The only time I really thought about God was when I did something wrong. I was afraid of His wrath and being sent to Hell. Therefore, I spent a lot of time looking up at the sky and apologizing while growing up. I didn't necessarily view God as a loving father, but a disciplinarian - He didn't really want to be involved with me except to discipline me. My natural father and my Heavenly Father were alike in so many ways, I thought. They only spoke to me when they were correcting me, but my thought was usually, "Where have you been all this time? Where are you when I am doing things right?"

I simply wanted a man to love me. I wanted to feel accepted. I wanted to feel significant and appear important in the eyes of a father. I figured that since the male figures who were supposed to love me weren't, I would find love on my own. The hunt was on and I was determined to find the love my heart was after by any means necessary. I was already a born leader with a Type A personality. Still, my father's absence and God's silence caused me to use my natural abilities the wrong way. God's silence is what tipped me over the edge. I felt God was too quiet and that He didn't care as much as His word claimed He does. I would ask for things, but they wouldn't come, thus making me wonder whether or not God heard me. Did He even want to listen to me? Did He care? It was like calling my father and not getting an answer. I viewed God the same way I saw my earthly father. I didn't realize that my image of a father was distorted.

The first institution created by God was marriage. God wanted man to produce a family, which consists of a father, a mother, and a child or children. This was God's original plan. Every person was to play a role in the household to ensure that it functioned as God intended. The family was meant to be a reflection of a component of God's character. While each person played a role and held great significance, it was the father who played perhaps the most prominent role. He was the protector, provider, prophet, priest, disciplinarian, rule giver, and visionary. He sets the order of the house, gives unconditional love, provides a model for God the Father, and plants the seeds of identity in the lives of the children. The mother is supposed to re-enforce the rules and the vision, helping to bring it to pass. She's supposed to nurture and help cultivate the identity given by the father. If the father was the CEO, the mother was the manager. The Bible says the wife is a help-meet. She is to submit to her husband's vision and help him carry out his mission; hence, the word "sub-mission," which means to "come under the authority of another."

She comes under the mission of her husband and then births and multiplies his vision. The problem, however, is that women tend to see submission as a weakness. But it is not hard to come under (sub) a man with a mission, especially when his mission comes from God. A man with a mission makes a woman feel secure. Submission is easy when a man is in position. She'll gladly come into alignment with his mission and fulfill the duty that God initially gave her. When a man is not in his position, the mother will be out of position also, and then you'll have the blind leading the blind. That marriage will be like a ship without a captain. Being that my father wasn't there, I missed out on the greatness both parents could have brought. According to the Census Report of 2016, 17.2 million children under the age of 18 are living in a single-mother household. Mothers have taken on the role of both parents, which she was never created to do. Because of the missing link, homes are incomplete, and children are in chaos. Broken children are having broken children and starting broken homes, continuing a broken cycle. We are a broken generation and a broken society that's mainly concerned with appearing functional.

Even the dysfunctional still function; however, they are unproductive and unable to prosper. "Broken children are having broken children every day, introducing an innocent child to a broken home, thus continuing the broken cycle. We are a broken generation and society, but we seem functional; however, we are not producing. Mechanical, yet, unproductive." Prosperity is holistic, not just monetary; it deals with the whole person flourishing. But that is not the case with most people today. When we are unproductive, we are not prospering as God desires for us to. God's word says, "I wish above all that you prosper and be in health even as your soul prospers" (3 John 1:2). When we aren't doing what we were created to do, we are not worshiping God; this leaves us in a place of distress and frustration. Things tend not to work out well when we're in this place. The women find themselves bearing the frustration of having to be where they're not supposed to be and do what they're not supposed to do because the men are out of place.

Have you ever seen a headless person walking around? This is what we look like today - a bunch of functional, headless women and men. Anything without a head is...dead! We are moving but unproductive because our head is not on our bodies. Because we have no head, we have no vision (no plan for our lives). When headless, we cannot hear; and hence, we're rebellious. When headless, we lack a mouth to communicate with, nose to smell with (meaning we have no discernment), and brain to think with (no wisdom, common sense, rationale, and logic). The word says in 1 Corinthians 13:11, "When I was a child, I spake as a child, I understood as a child, I thought as a child: but when I became a man, I put away childish things." Apostle Matthew L. Stevenson put it this way: "The process of a child is to speak first, understand second, and think last. But a mature person, an adult, you understand first, then you speak, and then you act." In immaturity, you act and move beyond your thinking, understanding, and experience. But what are we to expect when many people are grown and of age but stuck in arrested development? You know the saying: "Act your age and not your shoe size." Many people act their shoe size; they stopped growing and behave as if they haven't learned any better. When there's no father in the house, certain lessons aren't taught - the mother can only teach so much.

As mothers become the sole provider in the household, the kids are left to be raised and taught by the television, streets, even sexually abusive family members and friends. Because the mother is off at work doing everything she can to keep a roof over her kids' heads and clothes on their backs, they have to leave their children with people they think they can trust. Where there is no covering, an attack is inevitable. How many of you were molested by family members, babysitters, or siblings while your mother was away? How many of you were exposed to sexual ideas from television shows, porn, or molestation? How many of you gained a sense of family from gangs, cliques at school, sororities, or fraternities? Unfortunately, children are left unprotected and uncovered because the protectors that God created are absent. The first protector is gone, and the second protector, which is the mom, is also gone. She can only pray they don't burn the house down or get into something they shouldn't get into. The cycle of broken homes becomes a generational curse that passes from one generation to the next. The kids find themselves battling their fathers' demons; many of these demons are spirits of lust, masturbation, pornography, homosexuality, addictions, womanizing, and more.

A lack of supervision leads to a lack of reverence. If I raised myself, only I can tell me what to do. We hear children say, "I've been raising myself since such and such an age." We see children who are often being raised by their siblings. Many children are growing up way before their time, but what choice do they have? This was my life as a child. Listen, honey, I was grown before I became a grownup. I was playing house with neighbors, friends, siblings, and doll babies. Literally, at a very young age, my mother caught me breastfeeding one of my dolls. I knew that what I was doing was wrong because I tried to hide it. My father's sin haunted me because, at a young age, I had awakened love way before its time. This is one of the most dangerous things we can do.

The Bible explicitly warns against this in Song of Solomon 8:4. I watched movies I should not have watched, snuck guys into the house, and lost my virginity while my mom slept - she was too tired to tend to her kids due to working so much. I made a sex tape, more like a hunch tape with my clothes on when I was in my adolosent years using my mother's tape recorder. My mother found the tape and gave me the beating of my life. I knew it was wrong, but where did the desire to do such a thing come from? I was trying to imitate what I had seen on television. My mother tried to establish order in the house; however, she wasn't entirely successful because this wasn't her God-given assignment. While my mom became busy, I became the one who watched over my siblings. I had no idea they were watching and emulating me. Children follow the example of the one(s) they see, and I did not have enough sense to lead them in the right direction; after all, who was I following? Many bad habits were created in my youth. I developed some destructive cycles. Some cycles cannot be broken until the missing link is restored in the family structure, or there is some kind of intervention (Leviticus 26:39-42).

Let's break down the father role piece by piece.

God, as Father, created fathers after His likeness. He wanted them to model His likeness before their children. Everything God is, our earthly fathers are supposed to be; they're supposed to represent God in the home. According to Alcorn Kendrick, an expert from *The Resolution for Men*, "[God] did not simply realize that early fathers were like him and then decide to call himself our father. On the contrary, He eternally existed as God the Father in Heaven and intentionally created the role of fatherhood on the earth to reveal who He is and to show us the nature of His relationship with His Son." Every father is called to be a physical representation of God to his children. When a child looks to their father, they should see the qualities of God in a continuous and steady measure. Therefore, God is a provider, protector, prophet, priest, and friend; our fathers should represent the same. However, fathers make mistakes; they represent God, but God is the father of all fathers. When a father messes up, they're not reflecting God's character.

THE ROLE OF A PROVIDER

"Provider" is defined by Webster's dictionary as "one that provides." A provider supplies more than money; they provide in many ways for their children. The prefix "pro" means "before," so a provider sees basic necessities before the child even realizes there is a need. As a provider, the father lives in the future. A father provides time, energy, love, communication, a shoulder to cry on, tissue for tears, a roof over his family's head, clothes, and all other basic necessities. A father is supposed to leave an inheritance for his children and grandchildren (Proverbs 13:22). This includes generational wealth, property, land, businesses, wisdom, lessons, stories, tangible as well as intangible resources. According to a Pew Research Center survey from August 2017, the study examined the traits men need to be good husbands and partners. One of the traits was being able to support a family financially.

So often, young men are trying to support families when they haven't even figured out how to support themselves. These same young men often become fathers lacking a plan on how to take care of their seed. A provider plans for the future; they think about the needs their families will have up the road. As a provider, the father lives in the future.

ROLE OF PROTECTOR

As the protector, the father is the one that protects his family. He has to sleep with his eyes and ears open and be on the lookout for danger. God is a protector. The Bible says in Psalm 127:1, "If God does not guard the city, the watchman watches in vain." Psalm 121:4 says, "He who watches over Israel never slumbers nor sleep." A father sees what we don't see. Father God knows and sees everything. God is called El Roi; He's omniscient. With a father's protection, you can take courage, knowing there is no reason to be afraid - your father is with you. You know your father will fight for you, stand up for you, and never let anyone hurt you. A father would tell anyone that tries to harm you, "You must go through me to get to her/him." A protecting father will give his life for the safety of his children. A father covers his children with safety. Like David said in Psalm 91, "...under His wings shall He hide me." Sometimes a father's protection can come off as harsh or cruel, especially when we do not get what we want. A father might say no to protect us. Fathers know danger when they see it. Because they are men, they protect us from sorry men who possess wrong intentions or won't be able to love and provide for us as they should. They can often tell upon meeting a guy what he's all about.

The makeup of a father is different from a woman. He is built differently; his stature and abilities exceed that of a woman. They are generally stronger. According to *Father, the Family Protector* by James B. Stenson, "All the special features of an adult male's personality, developed from boy-hood - his muscles, will power, stamina, competitive drive, aggressiveness and assertiveness, mathematical and abstractive powers of mind, love for strategic planning and manipulating physical reality, strong sense of fairness and ethical conduct - all coordinate toward a single great purpose in life: protection". God has given men what they need physically and mentally to protect their loved ones. According to James B. Stenson, "The instinct to protect from harm lies at the core of a man's masculinity, and it is an immensely powerful force." So imagine when this is missing? The attacks happened because the protection was not present; it's like leaving a window open for an intruder with all the precious jewels glowing.

Men love to help; they help older women cross the street, fix flat tires, and so much more. A man's thinking is compartmentalized, making it very linear. So, whenever a problem arises, his mind is automatically geared to seek for a solution. Men fix things.

Men are hard-wired mentally, physically, and emotionally to protect those they love from harm. He is there to ward off danger. First of all, a family man devotes his masculine powers to protect his wife from anyone who would threaten her. It's the natural instinct of men to protect the women in their lives - wives, mothers, sisters, daughters. For instance, if a man were standing next to a man's wife in a crowd and some male stranger turned to speak loudly and angrily toward her, he would instantly come to her defense. Adrenaline would rush through his blood, his muscles would tighten, and his first impulse would be to rearrange the aggressor's face. No self-respecting man would stand by and let anyone treat his wife with disrespect. He would take swift action to defend her.

ROLE OF PROPHET

A prophet speaks for God; they hear the heart of God and operate as His mouthpiece. In the beginning, Adam was a prophet. Before the family came into existence, Adam was given instructions by God to share with his future family. God told Adam specifically in Genesis 2:16 not to eat from the tree of the knowledge of good and evil. "And the Lord God commanded the man, You are free to eat from any tree in the garden; but you must not eat from the tree of the knowledge of good and evil, for when you eat from it you will certainly die" (Genesis 2:16-17, NKJV). Adam received instructions from God and a word of warning, and he was to teach this to his wife and children what God said. The Garden of Eden was supposed to be their eternal home. Fathers live by Jeremiah 1:10, which says, "See, today I appoint you over nations and kingdoms (families, generations, house) to uproot and tear down, to destroy and overthrow, to build and to plant." When a father sets the precedence in the house, he'll uproot any lie told to his child. How does the father know it's a lie? Because he didn't say it, also because he has the vision from God.

Our human fathers will still get things wrong, but God's word never does. All gardens grow weeds, so it's a father's job to keep the garden and dress it, similar to the instructions given to Adam. A prophet pulls up any false teachings, uprooting belief systems taught in school or the world against the foundations set in the home. He breaks down all resistance and rebellion to God's word in his children's lives. A father teaches his family God's word and keeps them in the house of God. A father, as the prophet, builds the foundation of the family using the word of God.

Lastly, as a prophet, the father plants seeds of Christ's word. He is the messenger from God to his family. I believe if we saw more men in the church, more families would be in church, and the mothers would not have to force the children to come; they will run there because they follow their fathers. Children learn from their fathers how to call and decree things just like God did when creating the world, and Adam did when naming the animals. The Bible says by God's word, the world was framed (Hebrew 11:3). When a child learns from their father, they will not be consumed with what they see. They'll know they have the authority to shape their lives with their words, realizing that death and life are in the tongue (Proverbs 18:21).

THE ROLE OF A PRIEST

"As for me and my house, we will serve the Lord," as stated by Joshua in Joshua 24:15. He said that if serving the Lord was undesirable for other people, they could choose to continue serving their idol gods. But Joshua, operating as a leader, decided to serve God. It didn't matter that the land he was in was corrupt. Joshua knew where he was, but he decided to proclaim who he served boldly. He set the tone for his home as a leader, giving direction to his family. He made it known that God was the God he chose to follow. We all serve a god or the true and living God, whether intentionally or unintentionally. We were created to serve and worship something or someone. Being the leader of the home is synonymous with being the priest of the house. The priest of the family sets the tone for religious activities. As a priest, the father makes sure the family knows who the Lord is and how to please Him. This was important because people generally went along with whatever trend was popular, even if that meant serving idols. So the priest of God had to make sure people were following God and not trends; they also had to set an example for serving God for others to see. The father is supposed to model successful living before his children. He models the type of man his daughter should marry, and his son should be. The Bible says, "Train up a child in the way they should go, and when they are old they will not depart from it" (Proverbs 22:6). As Pastor Michael Todd explained, whatever you present before a child is the path in life they will take. The word manifests based on how it is applied, and God's word cannot return to Him void. So if you teach your son to love his wife, he will follow what you taught him; that lesson will not depart from him. If you teach a child how to communicate effectively and model it before them, they will have excellent communication skills because of what was taught at home. But if the environment in the house is always negative and filled with anger, rage, violence, and repressed emotions, this is how the child will act throughout their lives. You can always tell what was taught at home by the way a child behaves in a situation. Children are the therometers of the household, and the father is the thermastat.

The priest prays on behalf of his family. In the Old Testament, the priest would go up before the people once a year and pray to God. The priest knew how to maneuver in the presence of God and get to the mercy seat of God. He knew how to reach the throne of God and pray in the most holy place. Because of the priest, God would move in the lives of the people. When was the last time you saw a man pray? I never saw my father pray. My father did not teach me how to enter the most holy place. Books, the Holy Spirit, and adopted godfathers taught me this in my latter years.

The high priest went before God and made sacrifices on behalf of the people; he mediated between God and the people. The father, as a priest, brings his family before God in prayer. He spends time with God, laying his family at God's feet and seeking God for the direction and vision for his family. He prayers for the salvation of his children and God's mercy upon their lives. A priest intercedes for his family. A father covers his family in prayer, speaking against danger.

The first man in our lives is the one we, girls, look to as the standard of a man. In my case, my father was distant, so I believed all men were distant. Not only did my natural father act this way, but my stepfather as well. My identity as a child was cultivated by my father's absence, and I believed the lies the enemy told me. I was left uncovered.

Fathers were designed to cultivate identity in their children. So whatever the father is, the child becomes in response. For example, in my life, if the male figure was a father, then I was a child. If my father was a protector, I was protected. But if my father left, I was unwanted. When you do good, you are praised, but when you make a mistake, you feel less than. When the father acts disappointed, the child or children seek his approval. Children hate feeling rejected. Rejection has led to a huge identity crisis in this world. I hated rejection, and whenever I was criticized for a flaw, I took that to mean I was a mistake or failure.

God cultivates our identity by who He is and what He does. I am nothing apart from God. Here is a list of examples:

If God is forgiving, I am forgiven. God will forgive me.
If God is undefeated, I am more than a conqueror.
If God is Abba, I am His son/daughter.
If God is a healer, I am healed.

However, in life, our absent fathers create a distorted view of God in our minds. We think our Heavenly Father is like our natural fathers. If your earthly father is loving and caring, then God is that and so much more. If your natural father is a man of his word, then we perceive God as one whose word is trustworthy.

If my natural father would lay down his life for me, then I believed my Heavenly Father would too, which He did (John 3:16). When I would read certain things in the Bible, it was hard to believe because my natural father set a bad example. If your earthly father is harsh on you for making mistakes, you'll perceive God as one who lacks tolerance for mistakes. When a child reads how God caused Sulfur and fire to rain down on Sodom and Gomorrah because of their sins, that child will perceive God as harsh, cruel, and angry. Unfortunately, they haven't considered the whole story. They haven't considered where God was willing to do as Abraham asked and spare those cities if there were any righteous men and women to be found. God did spare Abraham's nephew, Lot, and his family. If your natural father was distant, you'd view God as distant, as one sitting in the sky, far away. But that's not God's nature. The Bible says, "God knows everything about us to when we lay down and get up, our thoughts from afar off and he knows where we go. Where can I go to escape your spirit?" (Psalms 139:7). The Bible also states in Acts 17:27, "God did this so that they would seek him and perhaps reach out for him and find him, though he is not far from anyone us."

There are many lies introduced to us by demonic forces; therefore, we must know the truth. But it is hard to know the truth of God when we hold grudges toward our fathers. Our anger towards our dads will cause us to not look to God as Father. What our fathers teach us through their actions, good or bad, is what we tend to believe. Like Randy Alcorn said, "Right now, this generation doesn't know what true fatherhood looks like. They rarely see it modeled in the media or at home". That saddens me because it is deeper than just an absent father; it's a generation who's separated from God. In the words of Randy Alcorn, "...deeply struggling to understand what God is really like." We aren't taking the time to get to know God; instead, we're allowing others to shape our perception of God. God wants us to get to know Him directly, through His word and through direct experience. God wants us to know him for ourselves. God does not want to be your grandmother's God, your mom's God, the world's God. He wants to be your personal and intimate God - Yahweh, your Lord.

Chapter 3

ARE YOU BETTER OFF WITHOUT HIM?

ARE YOU BETTER OFF WITHOUT YOUR FATHER? I am curious because many women I have spoken to claimed they were indeed better off without their fathers. Can I let you in on a little secret? As I mentioned before, the first institution ever created by God was marriage, and then family. This was God's design from the foundations of the earth, as explained in the book of Genesis. When God created this world, He called it good; He was also referring to the completion of the family structure. He gave the man and woman everything they needed to be successful and live their best lives. God gave the man everything he needed to worship, work, provide, and protect his family. He gave the woman the ability to nurture, and He gave her the divine ability to create just like Him (gone with your bad self, girl!). God gave the woman the ability and responsibility to be a help-meet and help the man fulfill God's assignment on his life. God told Adam and Eve to be fruitful, multiply, and replenish the earth; He knew it would take both of them to bring forth the world He envisioned for us. God made male and female in His image and likeness (Genesis 1:26). This means Adam and Eve were like God in many ways. Nothing was missing or broken in the beginning. Adam and Eve were perfect, complete, and whole. Satan came to destroy what God created, and mankind aided him. God's plan for marriage and family had been destroyed in the Garden of Eden when sin came knocking on Eve's door. Pastor Michael Todd preached a message entitled *Family Ties*. I truly enjoyed it. He explained that Satan didn't bother Adam while he was alone in the garden; he showed up after Eve came on the scene. Satan's goal was to attack their marriage, which negatively affected the family unit from the head down.

Satan convinced Adam and Eve that God was keeping something back from them. Satan wanted to discredit God in their minds by playing with their heads (the mindset, the way of thinking) and disrupting their peace. Adam and Eve believed Satan's lies, sin manifested, and death appeared (James 1:5). With the acceptance of sin, there was an orphan spirit released into the world. Mankind was finally separated from God, torn away from the source of life. Imagine being conjoined with another person, and then, you've suddenly been pulled apart from them with no sedative or preparation. Your flesh ripped apart, bones separated, joints ripped apart, and more. Imagine the mess. Imagine the open wounds that would be created. This is where the father-wound was created.

Were Adam and Eve better without God? Everything that God gave them freely, they now had to work for on their own. Were they stronger without the structure or discipline God initially implemented in their lives? A father's love was established in Eden. Were Adam and Eve stronger without God as a father? The father is the one who provides, protects, covers, and corrects. After they sinned, God told Eve that childbearing pains would come and that they'd be severe. Before the fall of man in the Garden of Eden, giving birth was a seamless process. Sin brought pain and anguish (Genesis 3:16). Sin not only made childbearing painful, but it made childrearing difficult. Sin made marriage hard also. The Bible says Eve's desire would be for her husband, but he would rule over her (Genesis 3:16). That phrase "her desire would be for her husband" actually translates she would desire to rule over him, and that she would struggle with submitting to Adam. This is a struggle most wives have.

God's vision for the family is a husband lovingly leading his wife and family, and a wife joyfully submitting to her husband's leadership; furthermore, both of them expressing trust and honor one toward another. After separating from God, a power struggle emerged; both parties sought to dominate one another rather than serve one another. When the Bible said the husband would dominate his wife, this means he will operate selfishly towards her, making it difficult for her to submit to his leadership. Sadly, his selfishness would make it hard for the wife to submit, and her stubbornness would make it hard for him to lead.

In his article *Her Desire, His Rule*, Tim Challies stated, "No longer co-equals, no longer different in function but equal in value and worth, God's judgment foretold that a husband and wife would now battle one another for control. The wife would consider herself more valuable than the husband, who would consider himself more important than the wife. This was the consequence of their sin".

So often we see this struggle in homes and the results of this is disunity, discord, and in many cases, divorce. This plays out when a woman refuses to submit. The opposite of a submitted woman is one that emasculates her husband. In the Garden of Eden, the curse is the root of so much of the evil we see today.

Selah. Take a moment and reflect on your own household growing up as a child. What did your family structure look like?

The worship of women as idols was introduced in the Garden of Eden. Adam's willingness to eat the fruit at Eve's request was an act of disobeying God. How often does this occur in our world today? Men have idolized women, and as a result, they disobey God. When there is no father present or the father who's present gives terrible advice, wrong perceptions of women become etched in a boy's mind, leading them to become womanizers to prove they are men, while others are taught to disrespect women altogether.

Before Adam outright disobeyed God, he was content with working the garden and enjoyed it. However, after Adam sinned, God informed him that he would have to toil while he worked for the rest of his life (Genesis 3:17). Adam lost the enjoyment of what he did. These were the consequences of separating from God in the garden.

As we can see, Adam and Eve were not better off without the Heavenly Father. Fathers play a huge role in the family. When mankind rejected God by disobeying Him, the blueprint for the family was damaged and nearly destroyed. This world no longer reflects God's original intent. Marriage isn't a good thing; it's a God-thing. Sadly, most people do it without God. We try to operate as families without Him. This is an impossible task. Marriage and family are hard because we've gotten out of alignment with God. When the Heavenly Father is missing in your life, your relationship with others, including your earthly father, will be negatively impacted. Many fathers are out of touch with their families. It is as if they have been misplaced, or are lost, without direction. Many fathers are seeking self-gratification and fulfillment at the expense of being dads.

After the fall of man in the Garden of Eden, our primary goal became satisfying our fleshly desires. If Adam and Eve, who were created as perfect beings, couldn't make it without the Heavenly Father, what makes you think you can? Some people make it seem as if there are more fatherless homes in the African-American community than in other communities, but that's not true. Many cultures and communities experience this problem; it has been broadcasted more among black communities. Seemingly, many Black men have been programmed to have babies and not take care of them.

Fatherlessness is an epidemic that stems back to Adam and Eve. Their curse transferred to their offspring, affecting all of us. The spirit of lust was also released upon the earth by Adam and Eve. This spirit leads us to sexual sin and sexually immoral behavior. Nowadays, sex is so casual. Its original purpose has been polluted. Sex was created for procreation and recreation. It was designed to bond a male and female together physically, emotionally, and spiritually through consent, causing them to enjoy a deeper connection. Many people, however, have a misconception about sex and use it for sport. Men who see sex this way tend to sleep with multiple women and produce children they're not ready or willing to take care of. I have witnessed this a lot. I've seen many women get pregnant by men that didn't love them and didn't want anything to do with the children born from these "hookups" instead of unions. These women are often faced with two choices: abort the baby or give birth to the child. Although adoption is also a choice, and perhaps, a good one depending on the situation, it rarely gets discussed. Many times, the males will encourage their female partners to abort the child because they didn't plan on becoming fathers. If we were following God's system, there would be no babies born out of wedlock. Everyone would abstain from sex until marriage. They would honor God with their bodies.

God instructs us in the Bible to maintain our pureness. Still, because lust is overpowering our communities, and many men are idolizing women, we've opted to disobey God and live for selfish pleasure. God's plan in Genesis 2:24 was for the man to leave his mother and father and unite to his wife so they can become "one flesh." There are cases where men are not leaving their mothers and fathers. Many married men are still clinging onto their mothers because that is the only parental love and support they've received growing up. They are afraid of parting from it. These mothers have become more of a significant influence in these boys' lives, far more significant than the wives. We call these boys, mama's boys. The family foundation is corrupt since the father-figures are missing in action. Yes, some father-less children go on to do great things in life and accomplish much. Even still, the deep pain of not having a father present can affect their ability to create and maintain healthy relationships with others. The boy who has witnessed his mother taking the lead role in the household might expect a woman to take care of him.

Without the guidance of a father in the home, based on all we've discussed, how could anyone assume they'd be better off without a father? Some say they're better off without a father compared to... Compared to what? What is the source of our comparison? According to *The Father Absence Crisis in America (2017)*, here are a few interesting statistics of how the family and community dynamics are impacted by a father's absence:

- 19.7 million children, more than 1 of 4 live without fathers in the home.
- Research shows when a child is raised in an absent father home, he/she is affected in these ways:
- 4x greater risk of poverty (poverty is directly linked to academic success which kids fail in without paternal guidance)
- 2x more likely to drop out of high school
- More likely to have behavioral problems (girls engage in sexual activity, and boys act out)
- More likely to go to prison – no guidance, discipline, rebellion, pride, wrong crowd, no fear of consequences

- 7x more likely to become teen parents
- More likely to abuse drugs and alcohol
- Experience maltreatment (moms who hate the father and mistreat the children). You can't beat a boy into a man.
- Individuals from absent father homes are 279% more likely to carry guns and deal drugs than peers living with their parents
- 92% of parents in prison are fathers
- Daughters are less likely to engage in risky sexual behavior when they have a consistent father

When a father is present, he instills a healthy sense of fear in the child or children and sets the tone for the home. Without a father, there is no morality. I remember when I snuck a boy into my mother's house, which I believe I would not have done if my father was active and present. First, I would have respected my father's position and role in the home and my life. Second, I would have understood my value and worth and known that sneaking a boy into my house for any reason was a violation of what I stood for. Third, I would be afraid that my dad would take his head off. Lastly, any man worthy of me would have respected my father's role and position in the home and would not have wanted to disrespect my dad by violating his trust and respect. But because a father's love was absent, my longing for a male's love led me to look for love in all the wrong places and do a lot of stupid things.

There were times when I felt unloved, and I went out looking for it. I knew something was missing, and my attitude was, "If I was not going to get it from my father,

I'm going to get it from someone else - in particular, a man." Although my personality was strong, the fear of rejection overpowered me in many instances. I'd find myself in one dead-end relationship after another just looking for a father's love. This became a pattern in my life. There were plenty of times I made a complete fool of myself for the sake of filling a void. Little did I know I was adapting to behavior and a lifestyle that did not belong to me. My father's absence contributed to my identity crisis. His absence spoke clearly to me about who I was and who I wasn't. It told me I was unworthy of love and commitment. I was dysfunctional in many ways because of him.

REAL CHARGE VS. FALSE CHARGE

You charge your phone to restore life to it so that it can last for a more extended period. But what happens when you charge your phone to 100%, but then it dies within seconds? That is called a false charge. The problem is the battery's calibration is not in the right settings. The same goes for an absent parent. It will appear at first that we are at our best, but once we begin experiencing the world, our battery levels (performances) will drop tremendously. What is the issue? We had a false sense of security, identity, and a wrong understanding of love. We appeared to be at a particular place in life. We seemed healthy and ready to take on life, only to realize we weren't all that healthy. We must recalibrate to the right standards and settings. God's original standard was to have a father in the home. When we live up to that standard, we can see ourselves and our situations authentically. If, however, we compare ourselves and our circumstances to another's that is broken, we may fool ourselves into thinking we're well. When a father is not present, we cannot see the actual battery percentage, we cannot see the lack we have and the issues we carry.

We must compare our lives to God's word, not our neighbor's situation. Comparing ourselves to anything otherwise will leave us with a false reading, one that causes us to say things like, "I am better without a father. I am stronger without a father. I turned out okay. There is nothing wrong with me. I don't need a father." Statements such as these are indications of a false charge; they're signs of hurt. People say things like this to cope with their pain and make them feel better about their situations, but that doesn't make these statements accurate. Numbing one's heart to the pain they feel doesn't make the problem go away. The true problem will continue to manifest in different ways and in different areas of our lives when not dealt with. It's like the "Whack a Mole" game - you hit the mole that pops up out of the hole, but then it pops up through another hole, and so on. You tried to suppress your hurt over not having a father, but it popped up in another area of your life. Most notably, this pain will show up in your other relationships, sometimes in the form of not knowing how to give and receive love and affection. Many times, this pain pops up in the form of making bad choices such as picking the wrong mate and staying in unhealthy relationships. If you don't deal with the issue, the issue will deal with you. Healing begins with YOU. We'll talk more about this in a later chapter.

Tell me why you believe you are better without him? Because no one runs over you, you are opinionated, you got your own stuff, you have experienced a little success? If you're better off without a father, then why are you still unhappy and unfulfilled? Why is it that with all of the stuff you've acquired, none of it can fill the emptiness in your heart?

Reflection

How do you feel when you do something great, but no one notices? What attitude would you have if you lost your dream job? How do you feel when no one praises you? How do you feel when a relationship ends? When everything is going your way, you feel as if you're on top of a mountain, but everything won't always go your way. How would you deal with the valley of disappointment and loneliness? What do you think about yourself when you fail or feel defeated? Do you feel helpless? Do you feel alone and like you have to do everything by yourself? Do you feel like no one is in your corner?

Many people are not aware of their real conditions until something happens that exposes the truth. Bad things in life happen to expose what is really inside of us. No, you are not better off today because your father was absent. You are living with open wounds and barely surviving. You are healthy when the original intent and purpose of God is restored in your life.

This book is not designed to help you get better; it's designed to help you become your BEST. My goal is to help you reach your destiny, God's place of promise for your life.

I want to see you walk in your full inheritance. But you will never access that place as long as you live in denial of your heart's condition and quote such bitter statements. To gain access to your divine inheritance, you have to be a son or daughter. When you are a son, nothing moves you; you are secure whether you experience failure or success, victory or defeat, make mistakes, or do everything right. Your identity is secure. A child from a two-parent home has a better situation, but they are not at their best if they don't have a relationship with the Heavenly Father. A daughter and son are broken when they are missing their father.

MY POOR BABY

In 2010, I met my college sweetheart. I had a dream about him, and suddenly, he manifest - the guy in my dream became the man of my dreams. I was 2 years into my college journey. I wasn't prepared for what would happen next. After about a year of dating, I got pregnant. From there, the dynamics of our relationship changed. He changed. After about 1 year of trying to get back to the place of loving each other, he stopped talking to me, stopped answering my calls, and started telling his friends I was crazy. I gave him a piece of me, and after he got what he wanted, he threw me away like I was yesterday's news. Not wanting to let the relationship go, I chased him until I ended up meeting another young man and gave him a piece of me as well. I was reckless. It gave me a high giving myself to a man who promised to love and always be there for me. My relationships (or should I say, "situationships") would usually start out good until it wasn't good anymore. Every man I encountered from 1994 until 2015 left me, including my father. They got what they wanted and then left me broken and empty.

The boy who got me pregnant was also broken. Like so many people, I was a fatherless daughter impregnated by a broken son. Like so many people, I was a fatherless daughter impregnated by a broken son. Why? I was like many women, lacking a sense of value and worth, and desperately longing for security and stability. This disposition opens us up to manipulation by men. Sex, for me, translated as love. I only had sex because I thought it would give me the love and affection I desperately wanted and needed.

like so many fatherless daughters, we did not receive security and assurance from our dads - and I believed the sweet lies and sweet-nothing whispers of a fatherless boy. Due to a daughter's father being absent, she is more likely to get pregnant at a young age, according to *The Father Absence Crisis in America Statistics (2017)*. Our security in relationships comes through sex and gifts. But as soon as these relationships get too serious, the fatherless sons run. Why do they run? They run because their fathers were the first examples to them of what a "real man" looks like. Their own fathers walked out of their lives when things got serious; therefore, these young men repeat what they saw growing up. Let me help you. When these guys leave, it's not because there is something wrong with you; they leave because there is something wrong with them. There's something they're going through that they're afraid to express since men are taught not to express themselves.

According to *The Father Absence Crisis in America Statistics (2017)*, women who grew up without a father are less likely to marry early and more likely to have children out of wedlock as teenagers. Without a father, we have accepted teenage mothers as the norm; we glamorize it on television shows like *16 & Pregnant* - that ain't cute. So many of our current shows present fatherless households. The next time you watch a movie or show, notice how they paint the fatherless child compared to the others. The world has proven that we are not better without our fathers despite what mask we wear to bury our pain. It is okay not to be okay, but you don't need to stay there. There is hope for you, and I believe you will become well soon.

After being hurt by the guy I loved, I became vengeful towards all men. I decided to do them how the men in my life did me. I got what I wanted and stopped taking their calls. I didn't want any man that reminded me of my dad, but interestingly, I kept meeting guys just like him. I sought out the men I thought I could "fix." These were men with potential but no fruit.

When you are broken, your life is built on a flimsy foundation. A flimsy foundation is not able to hold up or support the structure that is being built on top of it. This type of foundation cannot withstand a lot of weight and pressure. You are not better when you are built on brokenness; that is a weak foundation. When the foundation is weak, every outside force will eventually knock whatever structure that's on it down to the ground. The same is true in marriage. In marriage, when couples build on a flimsy foundation, the marriage is sure to fall flat at the first sign of trouble.

Do not marry until you have treated the fatherless-wound. If you think you are better without a father as a woman, you will undermine and trivialize the man you marry. You'll think his voice isn't as important in the home, especially as it pertains to the kids, because of your own personal experience. Except God builds a house, the people labor in vain (Psalm 127:1). Marrying with a wound due to fatherlessness is a recipe for disaster. You need to get healed before you decide to share the rest of your life with a man through marriage. God desires for your marriage to be a picture of his original plan for the family. A healthy marriage consists of two whole people becoming one. Marriage is not meant to cure you, but to grow and mature you. My wound due to fatherlessness made me feel every man would eventually leave me at some point because I was not good enough. My wound told me I was unworthy of love, which was a lie from the pits of hell. I pursued God, and He healed every broken place in my life. He reassured me that I was worthy of love and that I was capable of loving others.

Having a father-wound is nothing to be ashamed of or embarrassed over. The key is to get healed so you can help others do the same. You will have some who will look at you funny, but chances are they aren't whole within themselves. Because they're not healed, they'll deflect their negative self-perceptions onto you. Your focus should be on disinfecting the wound in your soul so that it will not spread to other areas of your life.

It was Satan's plan all along to deceive you into thinking you do not need a father, a covering. Stop believing his lies. He is the father of lies and wants you to continue to suffer in silence and be bound to your hurt and pain. I pray even now that while you're reading this book, you'll begin to feel deliverance taking place and the yoke of bondage falling off of you.

As I bring this chapter to a close, you may claim that

you are better off without your father. That's alright. But what about the rest of the world? This is a crisis. While reading this book, I'm sure you've started to connect the dots. Perhaps you now see how growing up in a fatherless home has disrupted your life in certain ways, especially when it comes to forming a relationship with the opposite sex. If that is your story, keep reading.

Chapter 4

I'LL ADMIT IT

AS YOU CAN SEE NOW, FATHERS ARE IMPORTANT. I was once asked by someone, "Do you miss your father?" I stared that person in the eyes and said, "I don't know." I didn't feel comfortable saying no. That would have come off a little too harsh. But at the same time, you can't miss what you've never had. Asking me if I missed my father was like asking me if I missed being a tree. I am not a tree and never have been. However, I do share a few similarities with trees, particularly when it comes to how our lives begin.

The tree and I both started as a seed, but trees have certain things I did not have, like roots. We were both cultivated in the early stages but, along the way, took different paths. As a daughter of an absent parent, I was missing everything needed to make me as strong as a tree. I grew up like the tree, but my roots didn't go down deep. During the early stages, you can't tell what a tree will look like because before it begins to spring up out of the ground, it spends much time developing roots under ground, in private, where no one can see. This helps the tree survive above ground. As for me, when my roots should have been going deep down, my foundation was unhealthy and missing the essentials needed to develop a strong root system. Trees have the proper soil to develop in, but that wasn't my case. When the storms of life came, I was not planted firmly. A tree with deep roots is immovable no matter what the storm brings. But at the first sign of trouble for me, I would completely crumble. I had many temper tantrums. I had absolutely no idea how to handle life. Everything moved me, I was easily offended, and relationship breakups completely devastated me. When I failed in one thing, I felt like a complete failure. A tree, born on the same day as me, is still standing firm, unlike myself. I thought of myself as a strong woman...until the storms came and revealed the truth of my condition. I'd taken on the identity of the problems in my life. I saw myself through the lens of my pain and hurt rather than God's eyes. A tree knows what it is; it doesn't suffer from an identity crisis. I, on the other hand, didn't understand who I was created to be. I took on the identity of my surroundings and circumstances.

A tree's roots anchor it into the soil; they also absorb the water that gives the tree nutrients. The roots hold the tree in place; however, my roots were weak. My roots had no soil to become grounded within. My family was my soil, but it was missing the most important element of all: a father. My dad was clueless as to who he was and who his father was. This is not to shame or bash anyone. I just want to paint a picture for you because in this chapter we are going to admit some things.

As you can see, the absence of these essential life qualities is the reason why there is a lack of structure and foundation. There is a lack of structure in government, in church, in schools, and homes. This lack of structure has tossed our world into a tailspin of identity crises. In the words of Apostle Matthew Stevenson, "Our world is in the midst of an identity crisis." Google defines an "identity crisis" as "a period of uncertainty and confusion in which a person's sense of identity becomes insecure, typically due to a change in their expected aims or role in society." In other words, the world's identity fluctuates with each new change. We thought we were one thing until something happened, then confusion stepped in, and we lost sight of who we were. We have strayed so far from God's plan for our lives that we no longer know who we are. Our identities come from our father. The word "father" carries several definitions, one being "source." The word "source" means "the beginning, origin, starting point." Once we get back to our source, our identity crisis will end. Imagine what would happen when a strong father-figure walks into a chaotic room. The entire room comes into order. Suddenly, there's peace and quiet. And he did not even have to say a word. His presence alone was enough to change the mood in the room.

If you have a father-wound, the first step to your healing is admitting you need a father. You must acknowledge that the way you were raised was broken. Ask God to reveal your life to you and uncover the areas where a father's absence negatively impacted your life. Honest confession is good for the soul. You must confess this inner need, this internal wound yourself. I can't make a confession for you; you have to make it yourself. Your healing is on the line. Allow God to reveal your heart's actual condition and do not be afraid of what comes up. It is all apart of the process. Admitting your need for a father will set you free from so many bondages. Admitting that I needed a father removed the burden of pride and anger from my heart. I used to say stuff like, "I don't need anybody," which wasn't true. That was pride speaking. That was hurt manifesting. I learned how to let go of that burden and stop carrying the weight of the world on my shoulders. Admitting you need a father allows you to give the burden over to God. Admitting you are mad at your father brings you into self-awareness, and this allows you to start the healing process. God told us in 1 Peter 5:7 to cast all of our cares on Him. I like to add to that verse, "...and He will take them because He cares about me." Admitting your need for a father opens an avenue for God to meet that need; it allows Him to become that father to you. Admitting you need a father invites God in to do the filling that you so desperately need. Honest confession and acknowledgment of your inner wound allows God to restore you emotionally and help you in life. Remember, the Bible tells us that "pride comes before a fall" (Proverbs 16:18). Scripture also tells us that "God resists the proud and gives grace to the humble" (1 Peter 5:5). So you have to drop your pride to receive help from God.

Acknowledgment is the first step to healing and transformation. We need fathers. If we can restore fathers back to their rightful place, we could reclaim our world. Knowing our fathers helps us to discover who we are and who we are supposed to be; this knowledge also helps us to gain a sense of security. Most of all, knowing God as our Father gives us the peace and assurance to live life confidently, knowing our Father loves us.

Next, we must forgive. Forgiving our fathers allows us to release any negative feelings we may have towards God and our fathers. If there's one father we need, it's God the Father. As long as we are mad at our dads, we'll remain in a place of bondage. If we cannot forgive our earthly fathers, we won't be able to draw closer to our Heavenly Father. If we don't have God, we have nothing. Everything we do will be in vain. If you draw closer to God while attempting to remain angry at your dad, it will be impossible because of God's overflowing love. If you feel you are not able to forgive your father, just draw close to God; He will help you and tell you where to start.

The closer you get to God, the more He empowers you with His strength and grace (ability) to forgive. We draw closer to God by releasing forgiveness and allowing Him into every area of our lives. This is the picture of real intimacy; it is where nothing is off-limits to God. Intimacy is saying to God, *I cannot love, forgive or release my father without you. I do not want to forgive him but this anger is eating away at my soul. I want to release this hurt so I can fully live, I need your help.* The power of confession brings freedom. God doesn't expect us to do more than we are capable of doing. He wants to help us transition to the next season of your lives. However, instead of releasing the weight, we carry it as a badge of honor. Holding onto the anger and forgiveness gives of a sense of control, but it is false security and unhealthy. The weight of these negative emotions is crushing us. Why hold onto these things when we have the option to be free and flourish?

Pride blocks us from walking in true son-ship naturally and spiritually. We block God and His resources, preventing Him from healing us and transforming us into who He wants us to be. If we did not need fathers, God would not have instructed us to call Him "Abba," which means "father." He wouldn't have sent His Son to help us become the sons and daughters of God. 2 Corinthians 6:18 says, "And, I will be a Father to you, and you will be my sons and daughters, says the Lord Almighty." The Bible also says in Psalm 2:7, "I will proclaim the LORD's decree: He said to me, "You are my son; today I have become your father."

God wants to be a father to us. Without having a father, you cannot be led, protected, or provided for adequately. Many times we are desperate for a father and it shows up in many ways. For ladies, we tend to date older men. This is one of the signs that you need a dad. If you don't admit it, your choices, decisions, and lifestyle will scream it for you. You won't understand what is truly driving your choices and actions. You may desire the right things, but with the wrong intentions and the wrong motives, you will always end up with the wrong things.

Any time a child is without a father, they are without a complete home, and they are considered an orphan. A home does not have to be a physical structure; it is simply a place where there is an assurance of unconditional love. In a real home, there is warmth, security, provision, guidance, joy, peace, and abundant life. A child without a father does not have access to these things; he or she is, in fact, an orphan. Did you know that? Think of this: he or she lives life as if they have nowhere to go and have no home. When a person feels they don't fit in anywhere, this is a sign they lack a father; they feel as if there is no safe place for them. A child is automatically an orphan the moment his or her father abandons them and is no longer there to provide, protect, and care for them. We aren't merely fatherless; this wound goes more in-depth, and it has a name: orphan. When there is no home and no father, we enter foster care. Even when it comes to God, we are walking around as orphans when He has called us to son-ship. We become sons (not gender-specific) when we choose God through the spirit of adoption and the blood right of His Son, Jesus Christ. You choose through admitting you need a dad, and once you admit this, you have the choice to accept the father you never had.

Admitting you need a father opens the door to Abba, God. God says, "Okay, you need a dad. Here is what you have to do: accept Me." You do not have to earn God's love or perform to receive His acceptance. You do not have to be the best. Thinking you have to earn these things from Him is an indication that you have the heart of an orphan or slave. God does not want you to be an orphan or slave; He wants you to be His child. Every human on the planet is God's creation, but not everyone is a child of God. We are only children of God when we accept God as our Father through adoption.

ADOPTION ANALOGY

Imagine an orphanage filled with children from different ethnicities, backgrounds, ways of life, hurts, and pains. The kids are on their best behavior because today is picking day. Picking day is when the kids get all dressed up so they can be presentable for the families coming in to adopt them.

Every child wants to be chosen. Every child wants a place they can call home. Potential parents come in looking for one child. They are observing the children as if they're items on a clothes rack in a department store. If the child is too old, they don't want them. They want a child who's younger and very cute. They look at each prospect's records to see their behavioral patterns. While the younger, more adorable kids get all of the attention, the older ones sit idle, being ignored. These children have to sit back and experience rejection every picking day. Each time they're overlooked and rejected, they feel even more unwanted. But then, all of a sudden, a king arrives. He comes in and tells the director, "I want them all." The director tries to show him the children's records and bring up their pasts, but the king doesn't want to hear it. He says, "I want all the children that are left. I want to take them home. I want to wipe their slates clean, give them a new name, and give them an inheritance." The director, shocked, fill out the paperwork. The children are all overjoyed. The king wants all the children, but not all of the children choose to go home with him. Again, they have a choice in the matter. The king says, "I want you all. Come just as you are. Leave everything behind because everything I have for you is new." He does not intend to leave a single child behind, but he can only take those who want to go with him. Only a small remnant goes with the king. The king didn't care about what the children did or how they looked; he wanted to love them and give them what they always desired: the love of a father and family. The interesting thing is the king came on a day when the children were not even prepared. They didn't have enough time to clean up and look "presentable." And yet, the king showed up with open arms. Many children who have been there for a long time believe this is too good to be true. Many of them feel too undeserving, and because of their perception of themselves, they cannot pull themselves to accept the new life offered to them by the king. They've always desired the life being offered to them by this powerful man, but they're preventing themselves from experiencing it. Thankfully, the king has an open-door policy where the children who chose to stay behind can always change their minds and take him up on his offer whenever they decide to.

God is that king! He is the King! He walked into this orphanage called life and announced to all of us who are hurting and have been abandoned and rejected, "I want you all. I receive you. I want to be your Father and bring you into My family. I love you."

God showed up! Daddy's here to take you home! Are you going to go with Him? He beckons us to have child-like faith because this faith simply believes what is told to them. Children are humble and understand they don't know what's best. Kids are not thinking, "He may let me down," or "I am not sure I can trust this." A child will run to a loving father every time.

If your natural father did not want you, God wanted you. He said, "If your mother and father forsake you, I will take you up" (Psalm 27:10). I know how hard it is to be overlooked in the selection process, but God does not care about your past. He wants you just as you are. He comes when we least expect Him to because He doesn't want us to put on a performance for Him. He's not looking for perfection, cuteness, and all of those other traits. He is simply looking for someone willing to let Him make them into the person He predestined for them to be. I told God, "I am never chosen. That crushed me so many times," and the Father said to me,

"You said you were never chosen; I chose you for me before the foundations of this world." He chose us before we even existed on this earth. You were chosen, and not last either. You were chosen the moment He laid eyes on you. When you were in your mother's belly, you were chosen. Not only were you chosen, but God also chose everything about you. The things you hate about yourself, God chose. When He formed you in your mother's womb, He chose your gender, height, eye color, ethnicity, smile, eyes, hair, and everything else. "Those of you who are rejected by men become beloved of the Lord," as stated by Redpath of the Blue Letter Bible app. When you are most rejected, the love of the Father is strongest in your life. If you have ever undergone the orphanage experience - of being picked over as if you weren't valuable - then you are in the best place ever. You're where God can pour His love on you as a loving dad.

David was overlooked by his own father and his brothers, but God had a plan for his life. Before Jesus performed one miracle on the earth, God opened Heaven and spoke so that everyone could hear Him. He said, "This is my beloved Son, in whom I am was well pleased" (Matthew 3:17). Jesus knew He would be rejected. He was the stone the builder's rejected. But He is now the chief cornerstone upon which the church is built (Matthew 21:42; Psalm 118:22). Rejoice even in rejection because it is a sign that God chose you. The world has no idea of this. God told the crowd that Jesus was His beloved Son in this way because He was reintroducing Himself to the world as Father. God had not spoken in 400 years since Malachi, and the first thing He tells us when He begins to talk again is He is a father. God wanted to show us He loves us not based on performance but the identity of just being His sons and daughters.

I learned I needed a father when God told me I had a father-wound while laying on my ex-friend's bed. I was crying because I had to come home to Charleston. I felt rejected again, but that was not the worse. I was sad because another of my relationships crumbled again after all of my hard work. I couldn't understand why this kept happening to me. Like tall timber, I found myself falling again. Eventually, I picked myself back up, talked to God for a few days, and it was back to my regular routine of being my own god.

Back to my situationship. I should have known it was going to crumble because this is the same situationship I entered into after God clearly told me not to. I was disobedient. God said no the moment I saw this young man at the altar of my best friend's wedding. I walked through the door, looking as fine as good wine, and our eyes instantly met. I received an impression from God, even though I was not following His way. God still loved and cared about me. He said, "Leave that young man alone." Unlike then, when I hear God say no today, I halt immediately. Back then, I ignored God's voice. I compromised, figuring God was tripping. I didn't know this man, so how could I judge him. Against my intuition, I decided to have a relationship with this young man. He showed me no sign of a commitment. He wouldn't even call me his girlfriend, but he filled the hole in my heart with the little bit of attention he did give me. I settled for this, but it was way less than I wanted.

Have you ever heard the phrase "emotionally unavailable"? This refers to someone who doesn't know how to show emotion and connect with others on an emotional level. My father was emotionally unavailable. He left my emotions unsupported. When children grow up with an emotionally unavailable parent, they date emotionally unavailable people. These people are always busy or distant and rarely in connection with their own emotions. They run from their feelings, and when you need emotional support, they cannot support you. My dad was far from emotionally available. He would say things with little to no follow through. And to my surprise my ex-situation was exactly the same. I had no idea how he felt about me other than what he said, and boy, oh boy, did those words not line up with his actions. If you are with someone and you are unsure of where you stand, that is your answer. Walk away. They will not be able to support you the way you will need them.

Let's say you're married to a man who is emotionally unavailable. You had a long day at the office. Coming home, you need your best friend, your husband. You want to talk to him and share with him your day, your frustrations and disappointments, but talking to him feels like talking to a brick wall. He has nothing to say, is unresponsive, and utterly indifferent towards you. This sends you in a tailspin, reminding you of your father, who was emotionally unavailable to you as a child. That described my situationship. I was in the process of getting my $200,000 three bedrooms 2.5 baths, two stories, single-family residence home when the guy said to me, "If you love me, you'll move up here to be with me." He promised we would get married if I left where I was and moved in with him. I allowed the enemy to play on my desire to get married. While God knows what we want, the enemy does too. He was promising me the security and love I wanted, but when I got there, we were dancing to another tune. I knew deep down this was going nowhere, but he temporarily relieved the pain in my heart. I left my new job and my family behind to get what I always wanted: marriage to someone I knew the Heavenly Father did not approve of.

Two months went by, and then the guy suddenly told me, "You have to go home because I cannot take care of us." Up till then, I was a wife without the title, keeping his house spotless. He just left me at his house alone like I meant nothing to him. I cried for hours. Ashamed, I headed back home empty-handed. After coming home empty-handed, I felt like a failure. He did not console me or support me; he was ruling over me. He wanted what he wanted, and I had to deal with it. I was ashamed because so many people told me not to go. I didn't want to face them and hear them say, "I told you so." I felt like I had no one to turn to besides God. I cried out to God during this time for help and direction, and He began to speak to me, saying, "You are not crying because of the relationship; you have a daddy-wound." The reason our relationships keep failing is that we have father-wounds. We have father wounds, and we are not healthy enough to be with someone else without running the risk of needing them to take care of us or nurse us back to health. I had no idea what God was talking about, so I pushed it aside in mind and got ready to come home. When I got back, I decided that I would follow God for real this time. I tried everything else, and it all failed, so I finally surrendered to God.

I got my relationship with God back on track. One day, while I was cleaning my room, God started talking to me about my father-wound. He revealed to me that I kept going through the same cycle because I was expecting my boyfriends to play Daddy. Many of us search for our daddies in our boyfriend. But the truth is, that is not where we will find them. Because of this longing, I'd apply a lot of pressure to each relationship, expecting from them what they were not obligated to give. That pill was hard to swallow. I responded to God,

"Okay, God. What do I do now?" His response was,

"Admit you have a father-wound. Open your heart and let's do the work." This was the work of healing God so eagerly sought to perform in my life. I had to admit the source of my pain and then open up my heart to God so that He could finish what He began in me. Open your heart to God today.

Chapter 5

MY LETTER OF CONFESSION

GOD TOLD ME TO WRITE MY FATHER A LETTER. Before I did this, God had me in a place of purging. I was purging from old flings, sexual relationships, and people I was offended by. God told me to write their names on a sheet of paper and burn the paper while releasing them into God's hands. I wondered why I could simply rip the paper up and throw it away; why God told me to burn it. I later understood why. It was because that way, it cannot come back and affect my life again. I did as instructed. I burned the paper and flushed the ashes down the toilet. Once I released the relationships and friendships that negatively affected my life, I was strong enough to conquer the source of many of my issues. I said, "God, what do you want me to do with this wound?" I wanted to be healed desperately because I wanted to be the best me ever. It was my time. Our fathers are not conscious of how they affect us since we tend not to express how we feel to them. We harbor angry in our hearts and burn in hidden animosity whenever they come near. Even worse, we try to play it off as if we're fine. But it would be best if you stopped lying. If you have an issue with your father, nothing will change until you tell the truth.

Please write a letter and release your father; release your anger over what he failed to do for you, even the things he may have done to you that were wrong. First, repent to God and release these negative feelings. When you repent first for not doing things God's way, He will open your heart to express and see what was buried fully, and this can be used as the basis for your letter to your dad. I want you to stop saying, "Why do I have to be the bigger person? He should be apologizing to me." Maybe your father is not in Christ, and you are, and you are more mature than him in the Spirit. God knows what doors forgiveness will open in your life.

Here's a prayer for you to pray:

God, I forgive (put your father name) _______________ in the areas he didn't protect, provide, cover, lead, guide, give me the template for relationships, and/or teach. He owes me nothing, and I release him. God, I receive you as my father. I accept your unconditional love, protection, provision, and covering. Thank you that you will never leave me. Teach me your ways. I welcome your Holy Spirit to comfort me.

In doing this, you are creating room in your heart and mind for God's healing; you're opening up doors in your heart that were blocked, thereby giving God full access. God wants to pour you out a blessing you don't have room enough to receive, but you have to create room in your life for Him.

So many people choose to keep their feelings bottled up, but whenever you shake a bottle and then open it afterward, a mess is made. Write out on paper what you are feeling. Don't bottle up these emotions. If you aren't confident enough to go to your dad and tell him how you feel, pen and paper is the best tool of expression. Just write. Don't try to be politically correct. Let your dad know how you were hurt by him, and you needed him, and then close the letter by saying, "I forgive you." You do not have to be a prisoner of your pain. The past is not your identity; it's just part of your story.

Submit your pain to God. The only thing He wants you to do is to choose to forgive. He will work out the rest, but until you let it go. God cannot begin the work of healing your soul until you forgive your father and all who hurt you.

I was led to send my dad the letter because that is just my personality - I like people to be in the know. I am a firm believer that we must be honest, and the reason why some things go on for so long is because of ignorance. We are destroyed for the lack of knowledge. In unforgiveness, we can be so upset with a person, and they have no idea. So how can you be upset with a person who has no idea of how they made you feel? It's like someone having a beef with you, but you don't even know it. They're harboring the anger while you're living like all is well. You won't know what's going on until they tell you. If you verbally expressed to your father how you feel, then I applaud you. He might take what you say to heart, he might not. It doesn't matter.

Your only assignment is to release it. As I will explain later, forgiveness is a must, but reconciliation is not. If your father is deceased, of course, you cannot give him a letter. In this case, I'd advise reading the letter out loud in front of a mirror or a picture of him. Although he couldn't prevent death, tell him how much you miss him and wish he was here. Express to him how much you hated living life without him, and how unfair it felt to you to do so. Make sure you get the release you need. Stop masking your feelings. Masking doesn't heal your heart; it imprisons it.

If your father isn't physically available, another thing you can do is destroy the letter in a fire while releasing him into God's hands. You can also read it to a father figure standing in the place of your father. Just get your release.

If your father is in prison, send him the letter. Let him know how you feel. Most times, people will try to figure out in their heads why someone is upset with them, and they'll be totally off. Only you can explain to your father what you're feeling and why.

I didn't admit I needed a father until I was older and much more mature. I misdiagnosed myself and thought my dismissal of a father was cool. Truthfully, I was vengeful, and I wanted to show him my hurt and pain. My motives were geared towards hurting my dad. Even when it came to planning out my wedding day, I wanted to show him I didn't need him. At my wedding, I was going to have the number of pews for my age. I wanted to show him a live representation of how I felt and exactly what I remembered. My biological father would walk me to the second pew, and then someone else would walk me the rest of the way, leading me to the altar. Yes, I had plans to embarrass my father because

I was hurt. Hurt will affect everything you do.

As soon as I sent my father the letter on Facebook, within seconds, he called me. I told him to read it first and then call me back so that we could discuss it. I didn't want my father defending himself or making excuses; I wanted to talk after he read the whole thing. He called me back, and he said, "I didn't know that's how you felt," and then he asked if we could go out to eat.

"Sure," I responded. We went out to eat and talked about how his not being there for me made me feel. He honestly had no idea. I remember a few days later getting a call from my stepfather. He told me that my dad told him how I felt about them not being present, and he apologized to me also. Now, they both knew how I felt about them, but I wasn't looking for an apology from them; I was simply releasing them and reclaiming my freedom.

Today, my father and I talk occasionally. I'll invite him to my theatrical performances and when I minister, among other events. But we do not talk every day. However, we are cordial. Sure, I could do more to grow our relationship. I feel that if someone really wants something, they will do all they can, but that goes both ways. I will always love my dad and I am glad that he is in my life. I talk with him candidly about things, we laugh, and so on. Still, our connection and bond must be rebuilt, trust has to be rebuilt, and comfortability restored. To pick up where we left off is impossible because I am an adult now. To do that, I would have to somehow reverse the hand of time and go back to the age of five. It's safe to say, that's not going to happen.

A heartfelt letter will open many doors, and so will his response. Your dad wants to feel important and needed also. Let him know his presence is still wanted if reconciliation is your goal. There are two levels of reconciliation: full and partial. We will cover this in the next chapter. In the meantime, here are a few prayers to pray by Beth Tucker:

FORGIVENESS PRAYER

Jesus, I thank you for forgiving me. Now, by choice of my will, I choose to forgive all who have hurt or offended me in any way. I forgive _____ for _____. I release each and every one of these persons into the freedom of my forgiveness, in Jesus' name. I also release myself from all woundedness, negative emotions, bondages, hurts, and ties to the particular situation that happened with this person. I release myself (by choice of my will) from being a victim of the situation any longer, and declare my freedom from all resentment, unforgiveness, anger, hate, and bitterness.

SELF FORGIVENESS PRAYER

Lord, I thank you for forgiving me for all that I have done. I now choose to forgive myself for these things and release myself into the freedom of my forgiveness.

Even as you forgive others, you must forgive you. Be specific. State their name and what they did to you that was wrong. This is a time of deliverance, so say it and breathe. Allow whatever has been lying dormant in your soul to come out. I would like to suggest that you also read the book *Pigs In The Parlor* so that you can gain greater healing and deliverance in your soul. I want to say "I love you" to my biological father and stepfather. You have both played vitals roles in the making of who I am today. I am forever grateful.

FORGIVENESS: CHANGING YOUR FILTER

FORGIVENESS DOES NOT MEAN "FORGET." Forgiveness is not a feeling; it does not happen when we feel it in our hearts. Forgiveness is a choice. Truth is, you may never feel it, which is why you must be intentional. Forgiveness begins with obeying God and making a conscious decision to release a debt owed to you by another.

Picture someone dangling in the air while holding on to a rope. At first, that person appears strong; they are making progress while moving forward, but then, their hands begin to hurt, turn red, and bleed. That is what happens when we hold on to something too long and so tightly. We start off appearing strong, and then, what we relied on for strength begins to hurt us. When the individual finally lets the rope go, the pain stops. There is power in releasing unforgiveness. There is power in letting go.

When we hold on to unforgiveness, what began as a wound inflicted on us by another becomes a self-inflicted wound. It will hurt more when you hold on to it. I know being angry makes you feel as if you have some kind of control over the situation, but this is only a false sense of security. I know keeping your distance gives you security, but control is the result of a wound. As long as you feel as if you're in control of the situation, all is well, but if someone crosses you, you'll resort to things like manipulation to get them to do what you want them to do. This is an indication that you're still not healed.

If you were not bothered by your father's absence in your life like you claim, then why are you so touchy? The fact that you still react in certain ways reveals the depth of your pain. When you let go of what wounded you, you are free to walk in the future God has for you. Forgiveness is not pretending as if you've never been wounded or hurt; it is changing your perspective in the situation so that you go from victim to victor. Changing your perspective changes your response. I want you to respond in a healthy way to your father despite the circumstance. If your father steps out of your box of control, then what?

Why should you forgive? You should forgive so you can find the root or source of your pain and stop it from growing out of control. Unforgiveness shows up in destructive and toxic relationships. Forgiveness gives you clarity so that you can see the true root of the problem and avoid cutting down the wrong tree. You must forgive your father to get healed, and God will show you precisely the location of the infected root. God does not want you to beat the ground and become stagnant; He will give you the tools to uproot that infected root in your life so your overall tree can return to a perfect bill of health. The infected roots must be removed or pruned so you can bring forth a good tree. The Bible states in Matthew 7:17-18, a good tree bears good fruit, but a bad tree bears bad fruit. A good tree cannot bear bad fruit, and a bad tree cannot bear good fruit.

An example of a bad root is anger. Anger causes more damage and gets nothing accomplished. Wisdom gets down to the nitty-gritty. Work smarter, not harder. Wisdom gives you intentionality and shows you the right spot to dig. You need to dig up the father-wound, but so often, because our vision is distorted, you end up damaging other good harvests like marriages, careers, churches, families...because you think its everybody else but you.

What are your automatic thoughts about yourself and about your father and your relationship with one another?

After I forgave my father, I received so much clarity. I discovered my father was the product of a father-wound also. It was my forgiveness that gave way to revelation. Unforgiveness is like driving with a dirty windshield, which hinders you from seeing the danger up ahead. This is a reckless lifestyle. Therefore, forgiveness is the cleaner that helps you see clearly to steer life in the best way possible. For generations, the fathers on my paternal side were absent. My father could only give what he had been given. I spent years being mad at my dad. You can probably relate to this. But the truth is absent fathers are just as broken as the child or children they abandoned. They have no idea how to be healed. They are only operating out of their knowledge. This became clear to me when my father called and said that after 40 years, he finally found his father on Facebook. He sounded so amazed and shocked, and I was happy for him. The moral of the story is when you are angry, it's difficult to show grace and mercy. Once I released my anger towards my father, I could see his brokenness. I was now moved with compassion for my father, understanding what he was feeling all these years. We shared the same heart cry that was silent, yet, life shattering, and no one could hear or see us because what made us cry was normalized.

We must forgive because God instructs us to. He forgave us of so much, so how dare we not forgive others. Because God freely gave to us, we can freely give to others. I also held contempt for my father's family and was carrying a lot of resentment towards them. I felt like they didn't show me much love despite my father's issues. When my aunt told me that I had to forgive, I told her no. I said I didn't care, although I did care. She told me God forgave them, and that I should too. I responded, "That's God. I am not God." I was bleeding all over the place and slapping a band-aid on an open wound that required invasive surgery and medical attention. Because I needed help - and if I didn't get help fast - I would die spiritually and continue growing physically. I would only age, and my condition would have gotten worse. This would result in me wasting my life and never reaching what God had for me. Without help, I was leaving a mess everywhere I went, a trail that would later lead God to find me. But does He not turn everything the enemy meant for our bad out for our good (Genesis 50:20)?

When you realize how merciful and gracious God has been towards you despite all of your flaws, this should cause you to be merciful and gracious towards others. God understands our pain. Think about it. How often have we turned our backs on Him?

BREAKING GENERATIONAL CURSES

Look how what the enemy wanted to use to harm me, God intended for good - to accomplish what is now being done: the saving of many lives. Joseph's word's sum up my life (Genesis 50:20). With forgiveness, we have perspective. I am grateful for my father's absence because it led to this story, it led me to write this book to help other fatherless children like you. If I were still angry, no good thing would have came from my pain because in unforgiveness, we are unable to see any good of our situations. When I forgave my father, God revealed one of the reasons He created me. God told me He created me to break the generational curse in my paternal bloodline. He shared with me that He sent many people to break their family curses, but they only became familiar with them and allowed them to remain. I was ashamed of the sins of my fathers. I never wanted to tell anyone what they were; I felt disgusting. One of the curses over my father's bloodline was incest. This sin visited me in my childhood. I hate Satan; you all don't even understand. The kingdom of darkness visited me as a child in my vulnerable state. Satan is such a coward, he attacked me early in my innocence because he knew why God created me. The enemy always attempts to take you out or stunt your growth in your early years. Why? It's because the enemy is threatened by your destiny, so he wants to take you out while you are in seed form. He is scared of your future. He does not know all God has planned, but he is aware that by you fulfilling your purpose, you will bring destruction to his kingdom. He would plant seeds in my head as a kid. Still, I knew that what the enemy was telling me to do was wrong, and it would break God's heart.

The desire for sexual pleasure had access to my life because of the doors my forefathers opened. I had a deep reverence for God even as a child, but I couldn't control my desire for sex. I didn't know who to talk too. I had no idea where it was coming from. I wanted to be a child, but somehow love had been awakened in me before its time. I never had intercourse with family, but like most of us, we played house as children. Cousins would come over, and playing house got pretty severe. For so long, I buried this, thinking, "How could I do such a thing?" There were levels to this generational sin because my father's bloodline actually had children with relatives. When God showed me why He created me, I engaged in spiritual warfare over my bloodline.

Forgiveness gives you the confidence and boldness to access what God has given you. I had access to the power and blood of Jesus.

PRAYER TO BREAK GENERATIONAL CURSE
OF ABSENT FATHER OR MOTHER
I decree that the curse stops with me. I plead the blood of Jesus over my bloodline; let it be infused with my blood. I decree that every power of darkness be broken right now. (Renounce your activity and familiarity with the sin and repent for letting it live with you). Now, I command all iniquity residing in my bones, organs, and blood to leave my body now, in Jesus' name. Iniquity, leave in Jesus' name. I cancel

every curse that resulted from the sins of my father. I declare that the righteousness of God is established in my life, and God's blessings are released to men and my family. Thank you, God, for your life, sacrifice, and truth that breaks every curse. I thank you, God, that where I was once barren, my life will now bear much fruit. In Jesus' name, amen.

Forgiveness reveals the generational curses so you can stand up and cancel them from your bloodline. Cancel the curses before you even have children. Say, "I decree that since I am the curse breaker in my family, the generational curse that has visited each generation is demolished. I decree it is destroyed from the door of my bloodline and sent back to the outer parts of the earth, and because of that, my future children will not have to experience it."

I need you to decree that whatever curse you know about, you declare war against it. You are the curse breaker for your family. Curses of imprisonment, teenage pregnancy, poverty, absent fathers, witchcraft, pornography, masturbation, infirmity, jealousy, lust, lying, rejection, perversion, and sexual sin can be broken through the power of Jesus Christ.

TAKE TIME TO FORGIVE YOURSELF

Once I realized the curse was from the enemy, I forgave myself. Even if I didn't understand why it was important.

You may wonder why that addiction of incest, anger, pornography, homosexuality, and more won't leave you alone. It is because your father thought he killed it by coping with it. He made friends with it, so it's visiting you. But not anymore. Not here.

The scar from your wound may be apparent, but the wound needs to heal. Don't ask God to take away the scar; the scar gives others hope that what wounded them doesn't have to hold them forever; they too can be free. Jesus is a living witness that you can be healed and delivered from anything, and He wants you free. You and I are extensions of Him.

IS YOUR WOUND HEALED OR EXPOSED?

There is a big difference between a scar and a wound. A scar is evidence of an injury; it develops after the wound heals. A wound can still be felt, and it's still undergoing the healing process.

It is vital before you walk in the purpose of God or the next season of your life that you get healed. Your future depends on your forgiveness because if not, everything will be felt through this wound. A wound will have you feeling like your body is hurting all over. You can force yourself into the next season, ill-prepared in your mind and emotions, but you will do more harm than good. Living with a wound will hold you back because it is not much you can do while hurting.

If you try to do anything for God while wounded, you can end up infecting other people who need healing. That is why it is so vitally important to check your heart before you minister to God's people. What is on you will transfer to the spirits of the people. You do not want to be a wounded minister, preacher, parent, or spouse. You can impart to others from your soul and leave them in a worse condition. Preaching from your soul is from your own limited understanding, feelings, and emotions. We must preach and live Jesus and wholeness so people can heal and not just cope using nice sayings. Before you go into the next season of life, you owe it to yourself and your future to be healed. Forgive your father for the standard he held over you that you could not live up to. If you have ever contemplated suicide, had an eating disorder, or joined a gang because you felt like you were not accepted, get healed from that father-wound. What you really desire is found in your healing.

FORGIVE YOUR BIOLOGICAL FATHER AND ACCEPT GOD THE FATHER

Forgive your father for providing the wrong example of what a man should be. Forgiveness brings you out of the lies and beliefs created in your mind. I believed every man that came into my life would abandon me, which was a lie. I had to come out of agreement with that lie. As the Bible explains, the world was framed by God's words. If we were created in the image and likeness of God, then our own realities are framed by the words we speak. We speak curses and then sit back, confused as to why our worlds look cursed. What you accept, that's what you invite into your world. I would drive men away before they even thought about leaving. I was so afraid of losing people I couldn't be myself, so I would kill myself trying to keep everyone else happy. With the fear of losing people, I would hold back so much of myself. I didn't express myself because if I was afraid to say the wrong thing and drive people away. I thought I wasn't worth fighting for, and that's why it was so easy for people to leave.

Let me tell you the truth. You are worth fighting for! You are worth the sacrifice. You deserve love, the kind where a person is willing to lay down their life for you. You are desirable - let them passionately and feverishly pursue you. How do I know? Because God did that for you.

The Bible says, "If my mother and father forsake me, God will take me up." I had to realize that although my father abandoned me, God accepted me. I had to know I was completely and fully loved by God because He loves me. I want you to say right now, "God loves me because he loves me." Rest in that.

It is hard to feel God's love when you are walking in unforgiveness. If you are still controlled by the father-wound, you will feel as if God can't love you because your earthly father didn't love you. But when you know that God loves you, you will realize that God loves your earthly father also. I could not live in fear of being abandoned by others simply because my father left me. I had to realize that my father was only human and that he did all that he could do - all he knew how to do. The truth is, I had a father, a good father: God the Father. He would never leave nor forsake me.

This was a hard concept to grasp, but I had to allow God a chance to be a father without judging Him based on my natural dad. Once you come out of agreement with the lies and beliefs of the enemy, you gain the ability to freely love, freely trust, and freely forgive. God wants you to forgive your natural father, especially in the areas he neglected you the most. God wants to be your father, your protector, provider, the one who gives you an identity. Forgive and release your earthly father.

NEVER AGAIN! THE TRUTH
ABOUT RECONCILIATION

Forgiveness is not the same as reconciling. There are three forms of reconciliation:

- No reconciliation
- Partial reconciliation
- Full reconciliation

I do not believe you need to reconcile with everyone who has hurt you or offended you deeply. The goal is to do whatever brings God the most glory. If you simply choose not to reconcile because you just don't want to, then your intentions are wrong, and this is displeasing to God. Let's go a little bit deeper.

We must forgive everyone that has hurt us, but reconciling with everyone may not be in our best interest. It might not even be the right choice or even be possible. Mark Ballenger of *Applying God's Word* states,

> "You can forgive people who have hurt you deeply, but sometimes it is not always possible or right to reconcile with abusive, hurtful, or unrepentant people. The Bible says forgiveness is a choice one individual came make without the consent of another. The Bible also says, however, that reconciliation needs two parties to both agree on forgiveness and the restoration of the relationship."

Reconciliation requires repentance with both parties and the desire to reconcile. Reconciliation is not unrequited and one-sided. The level of reconciliation is predicated on which is more glorifying to God and safe for everyone involved. God does not want you to reconcile with those still engaged in the activities that bring you pain and suffering and lead you away from God's purpose. God loves you and does not want anyone to continuously hurt you. Turn the other cheek means don't retaliate, but God does not want you to accept abuse. It is unwise to remain in situations that promote more sin and abuse. If that is the case, you will walk in resentment and hate God, wondering why He allows it and won't stop it. He is advising you, but there is something else that has your ear, misleading you. God is talking to you, giving you signs to get out of those unhealthy relationships! Just because you're a Christian, that doesn't mean you're supposed to subject yourself to abusive treatment.

My Christian faith is not determined by my ability to reconcile, but to forgive and treat others right. Love can be expressed at a distance. Everything comes down to the motive. It's best to ask God who you should reconcile with because He knows the heart of a person. He judges the heart. So, although the person may stop the abuse, what is the intent of their heart? Are they genuinely repentant and willing to turn away from that which hurts you? If not, there's no reconciliation here. If they are willing to do this, reconcile. Pray and let God lead you. This decision should not be based on your emotions but on the word of God and the Holy Spirit's guidance.

You don't need two people to implement forgiveness successfully. You can forgive someone in your heart without ever speaking a word to them. God knows what's in your heart. But to reconcile, there must be both parties involved.

Chapter 6: Forgiveness: Changing Your Filter

According to Matthew 18:17 and 1 Corinthians 5:12-13, it is against God's will to reconcile with people who claim to be Christians but refuse to repent of their sins after they've been confronted. When a person is still vengeful and a risk to you and others and living in a way that is contrary to God's word, forgive them while avoiding reconciliation. Keep your distance because they will continue to do the things to you repeatedly until it kills you spiritually and/or physically.

To reconcile with someone who's unrepentant is to endorse and encourage their behavior. According to Ezekiel 3:17-19, "Once you warn them, discipline them, and they still don't listen, the blood is not on your hands and you must move on for your sake and theirs." At the end of forgiveness, you want the person to become well, and we want to be careful not to love them to Hell, but rather, love the Hell out of them. We must not condone their sins, allowing them to continue in them while claiming we're showing them love. Love brings correction, and some people can only get better after experiencing a separation. God disciplines those He loves (Hebrews 12:6). God removes His favor and presence when people continue in sin. He does this to help them come to their senses. When God removes His grace, He is drying up the well in the person's life to drive them back to Himself. Mark states, "To reconcile with someone walking in unrepentance is the most unloving thing you can do for him or her."

If your father was abusive and he won't confess his wrong and ask your forgiveness, that is not a relationship you want to reconcile. If there is an option for reconciliation and you choose not because you are bitter, this is sin and a sign that you have not forgiven the person. Reconciliation is based on a person's fruits. If you see the fruit of change in them, proceed with reconciliation. The fruit is their behavior.

FORGIVE AND RECONCILE OTHER RELATIONSHIPS IN YOUR LIFE

We should always forgive and reconcile when possible. If you find yourself in an abusive relationship with a partner due to your father-wounds, move forward with co-partnering if it is safe for you and your child. Ladies, forgive the fathers of your children, and men, do likewise. Intercede for your child's father's soul because he is still a soul God wants to save. Just like your mother chose your father, so did you choose that man to father your children, whether intentionally or unintentionally. Pray that his/her soul would be made right and that they would develop a relationship with God. Pray that they would come into the knowledge of God. Draw them to Christ through your conduct. Show them a real Christian, especially if they don't believe in Christ.

You might avoid reconciling with your father if he is deceased or unrepentant. Forgive and continue to love him, as explained in 1 Corinthians 13. He does not have to come to your family functions, but when you see him, be respectful and say, "Hello." Until you are strong enough to go to family functions, stay away until God heals your heart. If all you can do is show them love, then do it in God's strength.

Partial reconciliation is better than no reconciliation at all. Sometimes, you may reconcile partially, knowing that the relationship will never be what it once was. Joyce Meyers' father raped her for years, and she forgave him and partially reconciled with him. She was able to lead her father to Christ before he passed away. She bought her father a home, which was a big feat for her; she was directed by God to do so. Look up Joyce's story. Her father repented to her and to God; this glorified God. She loved him and showed the kindness of God. She lived out her Christian faith, which led to his change.

Full reconciliation does God's heart good as well. I am the type of person that can completely forgive and move on like nothing ever happened. This may sound like forgive and forget, but it's not. That's not possible. I am not suggesting you try to forget anything, but forgive. But to fully reconcile, this depends on the occasion and the fruit in the person's life. If their fruit is rotten (i.e., abuse, mistreatment, etc.), do not reconcile. If a person has changed, it will be evident. Be a fruit inspector and allow God to give you the gift of discernment so that you can know a person's spirit. Was what occurred an isolated incident or something that happens repeatedly? There's a difference between a mistake and a habit.

If possible, after you forgive, seek to reconcile to the fullest degree if the other person is up to it. My father and I are working on our relationship. For example, we plan outings. I have not chosen to forget his actions, but I choose not to hold them against him. I was hoping you could come to the place where you will not use his absence as a crutch, as a reason why you cannot be made whole. Instead, go forward by choice of your will, and don't blame mishaps or make decisions based on the fact that you didn't have a father. As ask you the same question Jesus asked the invalid man at the pool of Bethesda, do you want to be made well (John 5)? The choice is yours.

PRAYER FOR ACCEPTING GOD AS FATHER

In releasing your father, you are saying, "God, I receive you as my father. You can now provide for me and protect me." You have to allow God to be your father. Allow the Holy Spirit to nurture you.

You do not want to be a wounded spouse, marrying in hopes that the relationship will heal you. To be a wounded spouse guarantees that there will be many problems, and this is the quickest path to divorce. What was supposed to be a picture of God and the church is full of emotions, tears, and hurt. You cannot be a good wife to a husband until you learn to be a daughter to God, and the same goes for men. You cannot be a good husband and father until you are correctly loved by a man and by God. You have to receive the love from a father to give that love. Also, daughters, you do not want to love a man who is not a son of God.

Men, we are calling you back into your rightful positions as the heads and leaders. If you have been irresponsible and lacking in your duties, go back and restore that relationship with your children while you can. They need you even if they can not articulate it. Let's break the cycle of brokenness and fatherlessness and get back to God's plan.

Chapter 7

A NEW TEMPLATE

BROKEN MOTHERS OFTEN CHOSE BROKEN FATHERS. But God wants to give us fathers after His own heart to love us the way He wants us to be loved and the way we need to be loved based on how He created us. The new template for a father God gives us is from his heart and mind. It is easy to receive this template because you have forgiven your father and received God as Abba. I needed a new template because I had no idea what a real father was like. I needed a physical representation of a father. I needed the earthly love just as well as the heavenly love. I desired for a natural person to be the picture of a father on the earth. In my healing process, I wanted a natural father to help me date. I wanted to know what it would be like to see a daughter fully loved by a father. All I ever wanted to be was Daddy's little princess. I use to compare life to television shows, but sitcoms like the Cosby Show did not hit home for me.

Comparing my life only confirmed that I lived in a fantasy because it was not my reality.

Every time I would see a father love his daughter, hold her, talk to her, I knew that was what I wanted. Dating for me sucked because I dated based on the influence of the old template. I needed a father to help me see what I could not see. We know love is not blind, but we will allow lust or our desire for something to blind us or paint a false picture. Codependency looks a whole lot like love through broken lens.

I prayed to God to give me a real-life picture of a father. My aunt then gave me some wise advice. She advised me that I could adopt spiritual parents. I then reached out to a father figure in my church. When choosing a father figure, you are choosing based on God's wisdom. Ask yourself, *how long have I known this man?* Does he reflect the character of God? Have you watched his life? How does he treat his wife? How does he love his children? How does he treat other people? These are all important questions to ask before choosing a spiritual father. He must be mature in life and he must know how to handle conflicts and his emotions. This man needs to have a wife so that they can model a godly marriage before you.

Even if you reconcile with your father, you should still seek a spiritual father. He doesn't have to be in your church, but local or close would be best so that a relationship can develop among you.

God is so amazing to me. He blessed me with many fathers. I learned that every man in my life does not intend to hurt and abandon me. I went to Jill and Treal's *She's Fire Conference* in Washington, DC, and one of the speakers was

Bishop Larry Jackson. That's my other "pops". He spoke with so much power and grace and made me feel as though I was one of his children, and he did not even know my name. He spoke on the true value of a woman.

All of the points he was hitting on almost had us slain in the Spirit of God. The power of God fell so mightily, and I felt the genuine love of a father. As he ministered, I was locked in. He shared how, when his daughters (he has five daughters) were dating, he would take their potential suitor into the basement of his house. The suitor had to lead him into worship. He trained his daughters on how to worship God, so he wanted to ensure that their partners could keep up with his daughters in the spirit. He said he didn't need a gun to scare them. Basically, if the man could not worship God, he could not marry his daughters. He also explained how Eve was created to help Adam worship; therefore, if the man couldn't worship, there was no marriage. He said a lot more, so I advise you to purchase his books.

I met Bishop Jackson maybe two weeks after asking Chris to be my spiritual father. I had to have them both. After Bishop Jackson finished speaking, I ran to his vending table, bought all his books, and stated how I wish I had a dad like him growing up. He continued to speak to me about a father, and my brown eyes just looked at him, hoping I could have him in my life. He said, "Take my number," and he wrote his number in my book. I felt virtue return to me as both men were getting ready to play a vital part in my life. God started this process of sending spiritual fathers into my life in high school and college. For example, I had another father figure named Pastor Otis, who helped me in these early stages of life. His wife and him are my godparents. I was at a critical time in my life where boys were a big thing, and I was skipping school to meet them. My mom was a disciplinarian, but she could only do so much with me, so she called for reinforcement. That's where Pastor Otis came in. His gentle touch on a senior in high school, heading off to college, was what I needed. At this time, he was the father I needed, and he would talk to my mom and tell her to be gentle with me. God definitely gives you what you need when you need it.

I choose both of my spiritual fathers, but I know God had a big part in that. You need a spiritual father to release you into new levels. I went to Bishop Jackson's church one summer. I was so excited to see him. When he saw me, he said, "There goes my girl! So good to see you" in front of the entire church. My father saw me. He affirmed the little girl in me. And in that moment, he reassured me I was seen and loved. It did my heart good to be seen not by a man but by a dad. There was also a time of anointing at the end of service. We were all praying. Service went on so long that my mom left, but I didn't want to miss what God was doing. I told her she could leave, and I'd take an Uber back to the hotel. My anticipation for God grew tremendously. Bishop called me out my seat and said, "Come here, daughter." He had anointed his hands with oil. He then anointed my head and spoke over my life, releasing me into my next season of blessings. He walked in the power of a father.

Bishop Jackson is my distant spiritual father. We often talk, and he has helped me understand some hard seasons of my life. I recalled praying for two young men to live, but they passed onto glory (died) anyway. I texted Bishop Jackson and asked him why did this happen, and he texted me back and said, "Sovereignty." He also advised me that when I pray, not to be emotional about my prayers but Spirit-driven. That freed me from focusing solely on what I wanted when praying and getting upset with God when He didn't come through for me. Bishop Jackson taught me the importance of praying God's word. He represents the priestly aspect of fatherhood in my life. After service, Bishop Jackson asked for all of his spiritual children to meet him in his office. We all lined up at his office to meet one another; it was like a reunion. It blessed me so much. It feels good to be included and accepted into the beloved of a father.

Chris helps me with dating, spiritual matters of life, helps guide me through the obstacles of entrepreneurship and decision-making. Chris supports me as he encourages me to step out in faith. I stepped out on faith in leaving my job and moving to Maryland. Elder Chris taught me how to worship God. I sang on the praise and worship team with him, so he always led me into the presence of God. He'd give me great relationship advice and spiritual wisdom as well. I remember I was dating this guy and, without Chris ever saying a word, I knew what his standard would be for me. Mind you, we never had "the talk." I gathered what I needed to know from watching his marriage and listening to his casual conversations. The guy I was talking to had a cigar in his mouth as his Facebook profile picture. I knew I couldn't introduce him to Chris because what father would want his daughter with a man that did not take proper care of himself? I knew this would be an issue; after all, we know who we can and cannot bring home to our fathers. I knew I couldn't bring him home. I remember having an entire conversation with Chris in my head. I was taking up for the guy, and I got mad. I got mad because I wanted my godfather (Chris) to receive the guy before they even met. However, I knew that to date this guy, I would have to lower my standards. I already had my doubts about him, and wondered continuously, "Can this be God based on so much of what my spirit is feeling? It feels uneasy." Long story short, they met, Chris was like, "He's cool." Mind you, I'm at the stage where I am dating for marriage, so this is serious. I was praying that God would reveal to me if he was a suitable one. I already felt a no in my spirit, but again, I often think I am being too hard. My aunt said she had a dream, and in the dream, I was telling her this guy wasn't the one. After her dream, the red light in my spirit and the head conversation with Chris, I told the guy that he was not my husband and that he could not continue in his pursuit. After about one week, Chris asked, "T, how are you and the guy?" I said it didn't work out. He then said he was going to tell me that wasn't for me, reinforcing what I already felt.

Some of the best advice ever given to me by Chris, my godfather, was, "If nothing ever changed, would you be happy marrying this person today. In other words, if you had to get a car as is without any hope of improvement, would you be happy? This is another life check. Don't marry someone just because it is a good idea and you don't like their life and their family, and you are hoping to change all that. If it never changes, will you be happy?" That eliminated plenty of men from the picture for me. If you feel you need to change anything about a person before you are level 10 happy or you thrive on potential, that is not the relationship for you. Chris prayed with me and so much more.

I had a dream about my godfather the other day. In

the dream, he was helping me get delivered from something I was dealing with. In the dream, he said, "You need to check in with me weekly; weekly check-ins." Three days later, he texted me and wrote, "Weekly check in. How are you?" God, as our ultimate Father, has a way of preparing us for so much, even the small things that we feel do not matter. Chris showed the protector aspect of fatherhood. For example, one day, I came to church with mascara around my eye. Chris then asked if someone had hit me. That was the love of a father on display. He that took notice and was ready to go to bat for me if it came too it. Don't get it twisted, Godfather was gutta gutta in the chuck. Lol! But he is a redeemed man, hallelujah!

These men carried the heart of God and have been phenomenal fathers to me. They showed me real love, how a father is supposed to love his children and his wife. They are my template for fatherhood. Jesus is my ultimate template, of course, but they show me flawed men can still be men after God's hearts. These men are my Davids.

God knows just how to give you what you need. When He says He will withhold no good thing from those who walk uprightly before Him, He meant that. These men helped to restore order in my life. They reinforced my value as a woman and would not allow me to settle for less than what God intended for my life. They affirmed and protected the woman in me God was developing. They guarded the anointing on my life and, as priests, interceded on my behalf before God in prayer.

Isn't it funny that they are all in ministry, and the same call on my life bears witness to their spirits and vocation from God? I had no choice but to be who I am. Fathers are like the bumpers on the interstate - they keep you from ending up in the trees. They are the forts of safety that help us remain in the will of God. These fathers spoke over my life, prayed for me, protected me, and providing me an example of Christian living. They helped to keep me accountable to God. I saw their marriages, taking notice of how they loved their wives and families just as Christ loves us. These men were great examples for me.

I am glad God uses special people to help us heal. I cried on these men's shoulders, and I called them when I was in distress; they affirmed me and covered me in the Spirit. Chris, Otis and Larry have all been the best fathers a girl could ask for. The Bible says we have many teachers but not enough fathers (1 Corinthians 4:15). Fathers are men who lead you to Christ. These men have helped me to grow in my relationship with God in one way or another. For that, I am eternally grateful.

Chapter 8

IT'S TIME TO MEET YOUR DADDY

WELCOME HOME, SON/DAUGHTER. MEETING your daddy could go three ways. The first way to meet your daddy is to see him clearly. We must move the face of our father off of God's face. The only way to see God is to move all preconceived notions, expectations and ideas; allow Him to re-introduce Himself to you. The Bible states only the pure in heart sees God (Matthew 5:8). For this reason, we spent an entire chapter speaking of the importance of forgiveness. If your heart is not pure, you cannot properly see God for who He is and who He wants to be to you. This process will take time because intimacy does not happen overnight; it is built through time. I thought that because I wanted God, He would pour Himself out on me, but He knows best. He knew what I was ready for and what I could handle at that moment, so the first thing He did was pour out His love. I needed love. Not a dictator, not a counselor, I needed a daddy. I needed a daddy to love me and console me. I simply needed a hug, and that is exactly what He gave me. Keep your heart open to God's leadings, promptings, and direction. This is a journey, but it is so worth it. Every minute drawing closer to God makes up for all the time I spent disconnected from Him.

Secondly, make an announcement or appearance. Daddy, I am home! This manner reminds me of the prodigal son - or daughter in my case. The story of the prodigal is found in Luke 15:11-32. There, Jesus talks about a father who had two sons. The youngest son was desirous of his inheritance so that he could live life the way he wanted. The father released the inheritance to his youngest son, although he knew he was not ready for it. The son left his father's house and went to a distant country where he squandered all of his money on wild living until he had nothing left and was flat broke. After he had spent everything, there arose a severe famine in the land, and he went from royalty to being a pauper. Too embarrassed and afraid to go home, he decided to stay and look for work. He received a job tending to the pigs, and he began to eat out of the pigs' trough. One day, he came to his senses and thought to himself, "My father's servants are eating and living better than I am." He decided to return home. He was willing to take the lowest position in the house because of shame and guilt. He knew what he had done was wrong.

I was the prodigal daughter. When I left home and moved to Chicago to be with my "boyfriend" at the time - the situationship - I left the security of a good job. I wasted time on the promises made by a broken boy. He promised me marriage and security; I believed him. I want to encourage you, sister, not to cast your pearls at swine (Matthew 7:6). In other words, don't waste your time on people who don't see your value.

I left home to be with a guy that promised me the relationship and marriage I desperately wanted. He promised me that if I left where I was to be with him, we would get engaged. He finally called me his girlfriend, but he still wouldn't post me on his social media pages. Although I knew better, I allowed him to treat me this way. A man will only do what you allow him to do to you. I devalued myself and gave my pearls to a man who couldn't care less about me. I didn't value myself, so he didn't feel the need to either. I figured that if I devalued myself, I could get him to love me more. I left home and gave up everything I had. I wasted all of my money paying his bills and ended up with nothing. I was too embarrassed to call home. My pride was in the way, and I didn't want anyone to question me.

I tried to make money any way I could. I desperately tried selling my furniture, but no one would buy it. I kept lowering the price, but no one would buy. I finally got a job, but my "boyfriend" then decided to kick me out of his home. He told me I had to go back home. I cried and cried. I didn't want to go back home because I would then look like a failure. Even though my best option was home, because I left against the wise counsel of my family, I was willing to do whatever it took to stay in Chicago. I tried to stay, but I couldn't find a place. I wasn't sure what else to do.

As time went on, I became convinced that God was closing the door for me to remain in Chicago. I believed my family and loved ones were praying for God to intervene on my behalf and bring me back home. Still, I was willing to remain in Chicago and struggle rather than go home and feel like royalty by those that truly loved me. I was afraid of being judged.

The prodigal son said to himself, "If I return home, I will be a slave, and that is fine with me. Everything is better in my father's house." I thought to myself,

"I'll be judged and scolded, but I'll take it because anything would be better than my current situation - having nowhere to go with my situationship." The young man even claimed he had to move because he was losing his house, which was a lie. After packing up and getting on the road, I literally had one of those moments where I came to my senses. I realized two things: As the saying goes, I can do bad all by myself. Also, I wasn't really mad at the guy because we couldn't be together, I was just fearful of going home and being judged. I knew I could do better than him.

I went home a little excited but feeling like a failure. When I returned home, I was welcomed with open arms by my family. I didn't plan to go back to church, and my confidence was shot. As soon as I walked in the house, my aunt said, "Pick your head up! You are building your testimony." She knew that the guy was lying about the house situation, and she knew that I wasn't telling her the whole story of what happened. But she made me feel welcomed anyway.

Just like the prodigal son, I met my father on the way home to my mother's house. My father was waiting for me the same way the prodigal son's father was waiting for his son. His father saw him from afar off, making his way home. On the way home, I told God I wanted to get right with

Him. He welcomed me. I repented of my ways and began to follow His lead. I returned home and started spending time with God, but I was still running from my home church due to shame and embarrassment. Then a friend of the family put on a conference called *Give Myself Away*. This was a three-day conference for women who wanted to rededicate their lives back to God, wedding style. There was a bachelorette party on Friday night and a wedding ceremony that Saturday and Sunday. It was a full weekend filled with white dresses, prayer, and deliverance. I did not want to be with any church people, I wanted to spend uninterrupted time with God. God said, "No, daughter. You have to be there." Still, I was refusing to go. God then said, "I have something for you. I will meet you there."

"Okay," I replied. "I don't know what you want to do, but okay." I had been welcomed home with a feast and the wedding of my dreams. The conference set up, but this was personal. Friday night was my bachelorette party; although it was a party for all the attendees, it felt like a party just for me. That night took me by storm. The presence of God was heavy in that place. Everything from the word ministered to the harmony and desperation for God and the ladies present was through the roof. When we left, I was drunk in the Spirit. God filled me to overflowing. OMG! That Saturday was the wedding. It was the wedding of my dreams. I recommitted myself to God and promised never to leave Him again. I vowed to do things His way and submit to His will. I promised I would live for Him the rest of my life and not give my body away again before marriage. Then I fell at the altar and cried my brown eyes red. I stayed at the feet of Jesus the entire time during the wedding ceremony, even while the other ladies were giving their vows. I was caught on camera in full-blown worship, dancing with God. If you've been at a wedding and seen the couple's first dance and the father-daughter dance, well, this was the moment. I danced with them. I could care less who was looking. Our song was *Press In Your Presence* by Shana Wilson. I completely lost it. It was as if there was no one there but me and God. These are the words to the song:

> *You call me your own, so Lord I give you me.*
> *You own the world, but yet, you still want me.*
> *Take my heart, take my mind, take my soul*
> *and never let me go!*

It was another day of me leaving out of that service drunk in the Spirit and rejoicing. I was so glad to be home.

Lastly, like the adoption analogy, the King came in, and He adopted each and every one of us, giving us the right to call him Abba through the Spirit of adoption. The last thing to do is to choose Him, not just today but everyday. Choose Him not just for *this* or *that*, but for the entirety of your life. Welcome Him in. Daddy is home, and when Daddy is home, order is restored. When I welcomed God as Abba, my life came into alignment. I was separated from friends and places. I was willing to give it all to God and break my alabaster box at His feet (Matthew 26:7). I gave up everything to move to Chicago, how much more to be with God? I gave God my life back; this was a picture of redemption and re-dedication. He didn't leave me even after I rejected Him. He was always married to me, so the celebration was a vow renewal. I got dressed, and I met Him at the altar in my white dress. I felt Him receiving me and welcoming me with open arms.

This wedding is what God had for me; this is why He beckoned me to come back home. He knew He was going to meet me there. But if I allowed my shame to consume me, I would have missed that moment with the lover of my soul, Jesus Christ!

When you meet God, you discover what's available to you. When you are His child, He reveals to you the promises and the inheritance that belongs to you. When you meet your Daddy, you get to know His heart, and you realize that not everything that happened to you was caused by Him. Satan came to steal, kill, and destroy, but God came so that we would have life and have it more abundantly (John 10:10).

I was finally able to explore a relationship with God without the hurt and pain and a distorted perception. The Bible says the pure in heart will see God (Matthew 5:8). The only way to see God is to have a pure heart. Ask God to open your eyes as He did Elisha's servant so you can see what you couldn't see before (2 Kings 6:17-20). Most times, God will attempt to show us things, but our eyers are closed because of fear, hurt and pain; therefore, we cannot perceive what He is doing. If you look back over your life, you'll notice times when God intervened on your behalf and blessed you. There are times when He shows you His hand, but you chose not to glorify Him. You may have taken the credit belonging to Him for yourself or given it to someone or something else. The worst part is we attributed many of the blessings of God to luck. But we know luck has nothing to do with it. We filter a lot through our experiences. Many times, we are not able to see God. Sometimes we misperceive God and our circumstances. For example, we may assume that everything that happens to us is a part of His will, that He willed and allowed these things. But it would do you good to know Him intimately so that you can know what's of Him and what's not so you won't blame Him for something He has nothing to do with.

I remember a quote from the movie *The Shack*: "Until you believe that God is good, you will blame Him for everything bad that has happened." That is a fact. When we hear bad things about someone, we tend to believe what we hear automatically, but when we know the nature and character of a person, we don't believe everything we hear so quickly. When you know God, you can discern when God is moving and when He's not. How much time do you spend with God? The more time you spend with Him, the more you begin to learn His character and His ways. God's love languages are gifts, quality time, touch, affirmations, and acts of services. God handles you and loves you through your love languages as we love Him through His.

When daddy is home, it's time to now dive into an intimate relationship with Him. He is the inseparable God that never wants to be without us. From the beginning, His desire has been to restore order to this fallen world, which is why He sent His only begotten Son, Jesus, to reconcile us to Himself. He sent Himself to do it for Himself. As the saying goes, if you want something done right, do it yourself. Intimacy with God can be pronounced as "into-me-you-see," meaning God has an up-close and personal view and hand in your life. When you are intimate with a person, it means they see everything about you; it means you lay it all bare before them, withholding nothing. They ask you questions, and you answer them. In Genesis, this is the opposite of what happened with Adam and Eve. After they sinned, they ran and hid from God. Once naked and unashamed before the presence of God, they were now ashamed in His presence. In other words, it sounded like don't look at me God, you won't like what you see. But God loves what He sees because when He sees you, He doesn't see where you fell, He sees the blood that He shed for you. They did not want Him to be disappointed by what He saw, so they clothed themselves. I call this the cover-up. When a person is exposed, there is nowhere to hide. Now that we are under grace, there is no reason to hide from God. He knows our flaws, shortcomings, mistakes, and even the things we dislike about ourselves, and yet, He still calls us closer to Himself. The reason we feel condemned is that the devil tells us how bad we are. He reminds us of how holy God is when we mess up so that we'll feel unworthy of God's presence.

God asked Adam and Eve, "Who told you that you were naked?" God did not question their sin; instead, He wanted to know who they'd been talking too. When our Heavenly Daddy is home, He should be the loudest voice in our ears. No one else should be able to tell you anything about your Daddy, and if they do, you shouldn't believe it unless it lines up with God's word. Basically, with Daddy being home, there is open communication, and we can be comfortable with Him. I know at my home, I can boldly walk in my mom's room; however, at someone else's house, I can't do that. I won't even feel comfortable in their parents' bedroom. God told me I can come boldly before His throne of grace so that I may obtain mercy and grace to help in time of need (Hebrews 4:16). Not only me, but you, too. It may feel uncomfortable at first. This is a new relationship, so that is to be expected. But become like a little child again and run into your Daddy's arms. He does not run out of love. He has enough love to share with the billions of people on the earth. God is not a human; He is a spirit. There's no need to think you'll be neglected by God when He is dealing with His other children; He can be with them and you at the same time. You won't be forgotten. You are not forgotten by God. He knows just where you are. He can't run out of love because He is love. He is not deficient or lacking in any area. I can go to Him in my time of need or when I am rejoicing; it doesn't matter. He never hides His face from us when we sincerely seek Him. He neither slumber nor sleeps. If I need wisdom, He said that I can ask Him for it and He would give it to me liberally without asking why I need it. He is at the door. Let him in. He is at the door, not just as God, but daddy.

Daddy's home. Daddy's home. Open the door. Let him in. Grab him around the neck. Receive his love. Sit on his lap.

Chapter 9

YOUR NEW NORMAL

L IFE IS A WHOLE LOT DIFFERENT LIVING WITH GOD AS opposed to living without Him. God wants to place us back at the royal table in our assigned seat. He came to give us life more abundantly (John 10:10). Without God, we lost sight of our true identity and took on the identity of the world. When we return to God, He helps us to live life anew - a new normal. In this new normal, I had to relinquish all rights to my life and learn to trust God in a place I had never been. I could no longer see God as just God; He was becoming so much more to me. I had to see God as Father. God is my loving and faithful father. He is my dad, and He can do whatever He wants with my life because I am back in His house, under his rule. I choose to be in His house.

In our new normal, we must let go of the things that keep us from seeing God for who He is: a loving father. So many times we hold onto things that are dead weights, things that hold us back and keep us from progressing in God. We allow all the bad things that have happened to us in life to become a brick wall that keeps God out and keep us in false security. God wants us to lay aside every weight and sin that so easily besets us (Hebrews 12:1). We allow these weights and bricks to become hindrances in our lives; they block us from relating to God on a personal level. We can't get past asking, "Why did He allow such and such to happen to me?" We have to see God as good, and whatever He allowed, He allowed so we could become better. We walk around carrying weights that God is asking for us to hand over to Him (1 Peter 5:7). Many people feel comfortable carrying dead weight around because it gives them a sense of identity. They have no idea who they are without that dead thing. Many people do not know who they are without dead weight - the weight of rape, the weight of depression, the weight of unforgiveness, the weight of loss, etc. We must drop these dead weights so we can enjoy our new normal.

We have to ask ourselves if we really believe we can have what God sacrificed His life on the cross to give us. Do we really want to be made whole? Do we love bondage more than freedom? We have to be willing to let go of old mindsets and lifestyles to experience this new normal fully. Idols must be destroyed if we're to experience this new normal. An idol is anything that takes God's place in our hearts (1 John 5:21). These dead weights are competing for God's spot in our hearts. God wants to reclaim His throne in our lives, but our dead weights have occupied His seat. We give all our time, passion, patience, and energy to carry these dead things, and we see them as things God cannot have or touch. We exalt them above God as if He is not big enough to handle what oppresses us. In this new normal, we must be willing to let go of anything that keeps us from God.

In this new normal, God wants to eat with us. He is knocking on the door of your life and heart and saying, "Here I am! I stand at the door and knock. If anyone hears my voice and opens the door, I will come in and eat with that person, and they with me" (Revelation 3:20). God wants to fellowship with us daily. If you eat daily in the natural and God says, "I will come in and eat," that means daily, we eat. He wants to eat with us. Daily He wants to eat and fellowship with us as we read and study His word in worship and praise. Not just those things but God wants to literally do everything with us. I don't know about you, but I can count on one hand the number of times I ate dinner with my biological father. I am not used to having dinner with my biological father, so for God to say He'll eat with me, that says a lot. He is declaring His desire to share His company with us. God wants to be around us. God loves our company, especially when He is welcomed in.

Slaves and orphans do not get a seat at the table, but when you are a son or daughter, there is always room for you at the table even when you are prodigal. You have a seat at the table, and your seat is right next to your Heavenly Father. If you make a mistake, there is still room at the table. Our Father does not give away our seats at the table. The truth is, a slave can never be a son or daughter. A son or daughter is always a child of God, no matter what. If you woke up today or tomorrow and you made the one mistake you were afraid of making, does that change your identity? You are a son or daughter not because of what you do, but who you are. What you do does not change who you are, although that is what is presented by the world. However, God is not the world; He is unconditional love. He knew what we would do before we did it. He is a provider because He gave His blood to cover every sin from yesterday, today, until the end of your life. It may have surprised you, but it did not surprise God. If you are an underachiever right now, having no awards to show for, or you're lost somewhere in the world, you are still a son or daughter. If you are not the basketball star your parents hoped you'd to be - let's say, you busted your knee and injured yourself - you are still their son or daughter. Even if you could never play again, you are still their son or daughter. Whether you are married by thirty-years-old or not, you are still your parents' son or daughter. If a teacher says something bad about you, does that change your identity as a son or daughter? Even if your parents disown or abandon you, you are still their son or daughter. If you lack money and success and even love, you are still a son or daughter. In this new normal, you must understand who you are and position yourself to receive from the Father. Your value system should not be based on material things like money, cars, clothes, women, men, and drugs. All those things are temporal. If they are instantly taken away, you are still a son or daughter. Truth cannot be changed no matter who chooses to suppress it.

God knows the truth, and even though I did some really crazy things after coming to salvation, that didn't change the truth of who I am. Our identity is not based on what we do or where we are in the world's system. Our self-worth is not based upon our achievements; rather, our identity and self-worth are based on who we are in Christ. I AM A DAUGHTER! PERIOD! You have to know this personally. When you make a mistake, you must understand that your identity has not changed. Even when you don't feel like you're a son or daughter, those feelings do not change who you are.

Your identity crises come from thinking you are an achievement, or you are a failure. No, your first identity is a son or daughter. When you were born, the doctor told your parents, "Say hello to your new daughter/son." Your identity is not tied not to being a doctor, lawyer, preacher, teacher, or sports star; it's not tied to your parents neither - to what they want for your life. The same goes for God. If He is your father; you are His son or daughter. Your identity doesn't change with circumstances. Bask in that truth. A child always has a seat at the table. You always have a seat at the table.

God wants us at His table so that He can talk with us. God wants to counsel us and give us advice, He wants to share His heart and mind with us and even certain secrets. God wants to communicate with us daily. There are times when you do not want to talk to God, but this relationship is not about feelings and emotions. The new normal is about knowing. Even when you are not able to feel or sense God, we have to know God is right here with us. Trust is vital in this new normal. If God promised to be with us always, to never leave us or forsake us (Matthew 28:20; Deuteronomy 31:6), we have to believe Him. These are the same promises we want from men, but these are the promises of God. God promises that in this new normal when things are hard, He is with us. He promises when everything is going great, He is there also. We can sense God in the good but not when our lives seem to fall apart. I remember feeling as if my life was falling apart. I could not seem to find God anywhere during this time, and all I wanted to do was be around Him. I tried talking to Him, but got no response. I tried going to church, but that was a bland experience. I tried singing, but I couldn't seem to make a connection. I can remember screaming at God, "Why won't you meet me?" I could not find my way into the presence of God. During this time, I couldn't sense God. I wanted to feel Him, to feel His sweet presence in the room. God shared with me that I was no longer a baby Christian who needed to live by my feelings; I needed to know He was real and that He was there. I needed to know that He existed and He rewards those who diligently (without ceasing) seek after Him (Hebrews 11:6) Even when you do not feel God, you must trust Him; trust what He said. After that, God gave me this analogy. My mother and I would spend a lot of time together. We would watch television until we fell asleep. I had my favorite side of the bed, and she had hers; I was on the top right-hand corner, and she was at the foot on the left end. My back was facing hers, and we both faced the television.

In the night times, I would have night terrors. I would be awakened out of my sleep in utter fear and panic. With my room pitch black, I couldn't see anything. But although I couldn't see or sense my mother, she was still at the foot of the bed curled up. God said that is the same way it is with Him. He said, "Although you are unable to sense and feel me, or even hear me, that does not mean I am not there." I had to feel around for my mother, seek her. But even in the dark, she was right there. God told us to seek Him while He can still be found (Isaiah 55:6). When we have to seek something, that means it's below the surface or below the shallow end, and it is not readily accessible. God wants us to seek Him and do so with all of our heart (Jeremiah 29:13). And when God seems hard to find, He wants us to continue to seek Him because, in doing so, He is repositioning us - He is taking us deeper in Him.

In this new normal, we must depend on God for everything. My favorite scripture says, "Trust in the Lord with all your heart and lean not to your own understandings, in all your ways acknowledge him and he will direct your path" (Proverbs 3:5-7). As a daughter, you should call your Dad if you need a tire changed; he will send someone to help you, just give Him the chance to help you. I know you are headstrong, and you can do everything yourself (or so you believe), but why try to do it all when you don't have to? As a single daughter, if you need help making ends meet, ask Dad; consult His word to see what He says. Ask your Father for a strategy and a wealth-generating idea. He is full of them, and He already placed inside of you what you need - that wealth-generating idea is assigned to your purpose. As a single daughter dating, ask Dad about men you date. Bring them before your Father in prayer and see what He says about them. Find out if Dad chose this man for you. Ask Him what He thinks about this particular relationship.

In my new normal, I would ask God about the men who were interested in me. God is the one who judges the hearts of men. It is we who look at the outer appearance (1 Samuel 16:7). With our natural eyes, we can only see the guy's appearance and actions, but God sees his motives. On multiple occasions, God said to me when I asked Him about a certain guy, "No, daughter. He is not the one." I had to trust God and not be afraid that I wouldn't find another one as amazing. There were times when I would push the envelope, but God is such a protector. He would give me a preview of the whole conversation I'd have with a guy I was interested in, and when the guy and I would talk, I'd think to myself, *I heard this before.* But God prepares us for things ahead of time. He reigns us in so that we don't get caught up in the wrong relationships. God gave my aunt a dream about a young man I was unsure about. I didn't know if I should continue to allow him to pursue me. God spoke to me about the situation through my aunt's dream just to show me how concerned He is with who I choose to date. Involve God because He does have an opinion; He is not silent. I used to think God was silent, but that's because I would not be quiet long enough to listen to what He had to say. We can't listen if our mouths are moving.

Children of God, ask God for wisdom and guidance on how to live and how to carry yourself. Ask God how to keep yourself as a man and a woman in a world where sex before marriage is the norm. God is the only one who provides us with a vision for our lives, and once He gives us His vision, we're to walk with Him daily and partner with Him to see it lived out. Ask God where you should live, where you should attend school, what church you should go too, and who you should marry.

God wants to pour out His wisdom on us, which is why He instructs us to ask for it (James 1:5). God wants us to ask Him and not be afraid. God is our Father, and whatever we need, He wants to provide. Yes, God knows what you want, but He wants you to pray and declare His promises with your mouth. He knows what you want before you even ask (Matthew 6:8), but God is such a relational God, He wants to see if you trust Him enough to ask for it. Do you not ask because you are unsure He can provide what you need, or are you afraid He'll say no? Don't be afraid of the Father saying no; even His "no" is a form of protection. As stated by Demetria Jackson, "A no from God is just as loving as a yes from God."

Perhaps you believe you will not be as satisfied with God's answer. No one wants to be told no. I get it. Sometimes, the enemy will make us think God is holding back on us. But you must remember that God created you, and He knows what's best for you even when you are not able to see it for yourself. That is love. As a loving father, He promised to never withhold any good thing from you (Psalm 84:11). Love says, "I want you to be happy, but I know that releasing certain things to you before you are ready will hurt you."

No wise parent would give a three-year-old the keys to their car, or their full inheritance at the age of twelve. Once we mature, we'll be able to look back and thank God for saying no to certain requests we gave Him. He knew that job, that relationship wasn't the right one for you, and that it would destroy you. He was protecting you. After all, He is your Father.

Another part of the new normal is taking the passenger seat and trusting God. God wants to bring you into direct alignment with His will. You must declare, "God, not my will, but let your will be done." The Bible says, "Delight in me and I will give you the desires of your heart" (Psalm 37:4). That does not mean if you want a cake, He will drop a cake into your hands; it means He will give you the desire to want the cake. He will give you the cake not solely because you want it, but because it pleases Him. Whatever desires

God puts in your heart will bring Him glory. For example, I was a sucker for men with dreads, dark skin, tall, and pretty teeth. If you did not have these qualities, it was a no for me - I did not want to date you. As I matured in God and began desiring Him more, He gave me a new set of desires. I began to focus more on the character of a godly man rather than his appearance. God put the desire in me for marriage, not to appease my flesh but to bring Him glory. God had to change my heart, and I had to allow Him to do so. Until you allow God to change your heart, you will continue to be a brat and get upset every time you don't get what you want. Sometimes our standards are too low, and God is telling us to come up higher. He wants to give us the best and to show us what you have access to in Him. Appearances are good, but it's not the most important thing, nor is it more important than a person's character and relationship with God. If I found the guy I once desired, I would have compromised my walk with God and neglected to seek God for His best. I would have settled, thinking I had God's best, not knowing I didn't. God wants the best for us, but we must desire what He wants over what we want.

God's will for us is to submit our lives to Him. God shouldn't have to take the wheel forcefully; you should humbly give it to Him. Before you do anything, you should consider the Father's heart first. You should acknowledge Him first, and then ask Him to guide you. Your prayer life changes when you focus on God's will and make it your priority. Your prayer life will grow and become more effective.

We pray to God because we understand who He is, and we acknowledge what He is capable of. What a privilege it is to pray and call the Creator of the universe "Daddy."

Most people run to God after they've made a mess, hoping He'd clean it up for them. Many times, we will make all of the wrong decisions because we refuse to ask God first, and then, only afterward do we pray. Furthermore, when we pray, God will give us an answer that unravels all of our plans and desires, causing us to start over. I have been there many times. I've asked God to bless what He never intended for me to have. I heard a saying once, "God is not obligated to pay for what He did not order." We ask God to bless relationships and businesses on the back end, whereas He was not consulted in the beginning. Living in this new normal is learning to put God first in everything.

Matthew 6:33 says, "Seek ye first the Kingdom of God and all ways of doing and being right, and then everything else will be added unto you." God says, "Heathens, those who are not his children, are concerned about what they will eat, what they will wear, and what they will drink." Basically, God is saying, "I am a good dad. I don't need to be reminded of the needs of my children." The Bible says God takes care of the birds who neither store up, nor do they save - He simply feeds them. How much more will He take care of you (Matthew 6:26-34)?

In this new normal, it is vital to learn the language of the Father. God's language is His word. We must learn the basic instructions before leaving earth. The word of God is how we should live. If God's word is the way, the truth, and the life, then why not study what will help us live in the new normal, which is the life of the Kingdom of God? The will of God is the language of this new normal, and faith is the currency that brings what we need out of the Kingdom of God into the natural realm. Faith pleases God, and without faith, it is impossible to please God (Hebrews 11:6). The question, however, is how you can please someone you do not trust?

In communication with God, the Bible says, "This is the confidence we have in approaching God: that if we ask anything according to his will, he hears us. And if we know that he hears us—whatever we ask—we know that we have what we asked of him" (1 John 5:14). God moves according to his word. If we speak His will, which is his word, then we know He hears us and will do what we ask. This is the confidence we have in approaching God; this is how we can approach our Dad in Heaven while on the earth. You want to make the earth move and experience life as it is lived in Heaven, then speak the language of God, which is his word, His will. You want to see prayers answered, develop a relationship with God, and speak what He wants to see. His word will not return to Him void; it will manifest in your life when spoken. We tend to pray according to our will, and when nothing happens, we get upset. The reason nothing happens is that we are praying another language - we are praying using the world's language (kingdom; system). The language of this new normal is the word and purpose of God. When other people come to discover this new normal, we have a mandate to teach them the language of God and demonstrate before them this new normal.

We need to understand this language, not only speak it. We are bringing an unfamiliar language to an established world, and this world is loud. Unless you know this language, you will not be able to distinguish God's voice from the voices of the world or your flesh. God stated in John 10:27, "My sheep know my voice, and I know them and the voice of a stranger they will not follow." Do not be led astray by the things in this natural realm and the lies the enemy tells.

God, as Abba, Father, never means us any harm; He never intends to hurt us. Sometimes I am still unsure how to approach God about things. I over-think things a lot, but God is like, "Just come. Don't worry about perfection." As Abba, He says we can talk to Him about anything. What makes God a friend is we can come to Him at any time, and He is always available to us. We can sit on His lap or lay our heads on His shoulder.

A daddy's girl is favored by her father and totally and completely loved. I remember God asked me, "If we are in the house together, why is that when you get up, you don't speak?" When you are a daddy's girl, your dad is the first person you run to for love. You say, "Good morning, daddy!" You're just glad to be in his presence and in his face. In the new normal, when I arise in the morning, the first thing I do is speak to my Dad - after all, it is He who woke me up. I made it a habit of envisioning God coming into my room and nudging me to get up. Neither the alarm clock or the loud noises outside wake us up; it is God who wakes us up and decides to give us another day to live.

I started living every day as if the Lord walks and lives with me. For example, I don't simply think that the food I eat is what I cooked or my mom prepared, I say thank you, Father, for this food because He provided it. We simply prepared it. If it had not been for His creations - chickens, cow, and pigs - we would not be able to eat these things. I find ways to trace everything back to God because everything is His according to the word (John 1:3). I am thankful to have His blessings. When I say grace over my food, I'm not merely thanking God for the meal that's before me; I am thanking God for making the food we consume. I thank Him for safely getting me everywhere that I need to go. He keeps me from dangers seen and unseen. I didn't get there alone. The enemy is always trying to take us out. Thank God for keeping you because if His eyes are not on the city, the watchman watches in vain (Psalm 127:1).

My new normal is being patient with the new relationship I have with God. I thought at first that I would magically be so close with God, and He'd be putting in all the work. I was waiting for Him just to create this relationship, and I just live in it, but it takes two to tangle. He meets us when we draw nigh unto Him (James 4:8). This relationship is like any other relationship in our lives - it requires time and energy to grow.

My new normal is living out the plan of the Father's heart. Even good parents have plans for their children. They want to see their children live out their plans and not walk in rebellion. The same goes for God. As our good Father, He had a plan for you before you were born (Psalm 139:6), and He wants you to walk in it. After I surrendered to God that day in February of 2015 - at my wedding ceremony - my sense of purpose was finally awakened. I fully surrendered to the plan of God. I was now clear on what I was created to do. I was finally free to walk in my purpose, no longer held back by my past. I no longer live in fear because I understand who walks with me. My Daddy is with me, so whom shall I fear? Greater is He that is inside of me than he that is in the world (1 John 4:4). If your father is in the house, he is your protector.

With God living with me, there are no more closed

doors - no more doing things in private. God definitely wants to expose what is done in the dark because He does not want you living a secret life. He wants you to live boldly for Him both privately and publicly.

When a door is closed, no one can see what is happening, but when it's open, there is nothing hidden. I live my life openly before God. There are no restricted areas in my heart. You close doors when you don't want people in certain areas or if you are doing something that you don't have any business doing. But I want God in every area of me. I want Him to roam freely and not feel like a guest in His own house.

What I mean by "God in the house" is His presence is accessible to me. God's presence is His face made known. If His face is with us, that means His ears, mouth, and eyes are too. In other words, whatever you do, God is doing it with you, or you make Him watch even when He does not want too. I no longer watch certain shows, listen to certain music, and go to certain places. In this new normal, it is all about pleasing God. Jesus said in John 8:9, "...for I always do what pleases Him (the Father)." I don't always get it right, but the good thing about being a child of God is I forever belong to Him. I am never separated from His love. Mistakes are doorways to His correction and love.

The new normal is a life of worship, not just on Sundays but every day. Keeping God on your mind helps us to thank Him in everything and stay in a posture of worship. Worship is more than singing songs on a Sunday morning; it is a lifestyle. Worship is how you treat others, including those that can't do anything for you. Worship is being at work and working as unto the glory of God (1 Corinthians 10:31). Worship is spending more time with God, more than anything else. Worship is your thoughts - do they glorify God? Does your conversation glorify God? Does your marriage glorify God? Do the things you do in secret please God? Can God happily dwell in you throughout your daily life? Or would the Spirit of God be grieved? Living with God, many things in your life will have to change because whenever you love someone, you do what pleases them regardless of what you want. Love is self-sacrificing. Ask God to give you a hatred for the things He hates and a love for the things He loves.

My Dad expressed to me that I shouldn't watch movies and shows that awaken love and arouse sexual desires. Is that a movie you would watch with your dad? He also reminded me that I wouldn't condone these sins with my friends, so why would I watch them and put that kind of trash in my spirit? I had to give up the drama that brought me joy but planted sinful seeds in my spirit.

I desperately desired to know God more and grow in our relationship and in my gifts. I wanted to know how I could hear God more accurately and tap into my prophetic gift. Being around so many prophetic people stirred this curiosity within me. During one church service, I asked a young lady how to walk in the prophetic. She explained that I could no longer live casually. Basically, to experience God on a greater level, I could not live like everyone else. I had to live on a higher level, called out and set apart. I had to guard my eyes, ears, and mouth. These are the gateways to my spirit. I had to make sure my spirit did not get contaminated by the things of the world. I had to de-clutter my spirit and mind and stop living according to the trends of the day. It was no longer about popular opinion, but God's opinion. I also had to shut out a lot of voices in my life in this new normal. Being in this new normal is about giving God your ears.

I had to draw a line in the sand on what I could and could not do and entertain. In other words, I had to enter into consecration. Consecration purifies you, and as I stated before, the pure in heart see God (Matthew 5:8). In consecration, God cleans us out so our filters can be clear. Whenever God wants to take you higher, He always separates you and calls you out from among the crowd.

The new normal entails involving God in everything; this means more consecration, shutting off the world, and focusing on God. I had to dethrone idols and the things that took my attention away from God.

So, you don't know what to give up? Give up whatever takes your heart away from God, whatever you spend more time with than God. Television. Relationships. Friendships. Desires (even godly ones). Even when it comes to work, make sure you spend time with God. Pray about working on Sundays and during Bible Study nights. If you have a hectic schedule, then listen to the Bible and sermons using Apps on your phone or on the computer. On the days you are off, spend time studying God's word, and fellowshipping with Him in prayer. He will bless you with a job where you can spend more time with Him even while making more money. Whatever season you are in, ask God to make you a good steward. If you aren't a good steward over the time you have now, what will you do with more? I remember saying, "God, I don't have time to spend with you," and God responded,

"The problem is not having time; the issue is you're

not making time. You make time for everything else." He then asked me, "How can you say you don't have time, and yet, you spent so much time watching television every day?" In this new normal, you must turn the tables. If you spent three hours watching television, take one of those hours and spend it with God. Apostle Matthew Stevenson put it this way: "Kill that thing, not sacrifice it. If there is anything in my life that I feel separates me from God, if I even feel it is an issue, cut it off. Suffer nothing to live."

The new normal is a great place; its better than any other norm imposed upon you. In spending time with God, don't over-think things or make them complicated. There is no checklist. Spend time with God as you would do with someone you were dating. Get to know God. When you watched television, you weren't wondering if you were doing this or that right; you just enjoyed your time with that individual. It is the same thing with God. Just enjoy His presence. Enjoy being with Him. Spend time watching sermons and reading the Bible. Discipline yourself to spend time with Him. Don't be like Martha, who was so concerned with all of the details - "Is this long enough? Should I pray this long? Should I go to this many services? How many scriptures should I read?" Instead, be like Mary. She was focused on being close to Jesus, enjoying His presence while sitting at His feet. Don't focus so much on the details that you miss the relationship. This may be a difficult habit to break because the enemy does not want you to draw closer to God. He will try to put up a wall on every front. Those walls (strongholds) don't mean that God does not want to spend time with you; they are a sign that it's time to engage in spiritual warfare. You have to fight back against what the enemy is doing to sabotage your walk with God. How do you fight back? With the word of God. Like Paul declared, we must beat our bodies into submission to God (1 Corinthians 9:27). Your body is doing something it has never done before. Your flesh is uncomfortable because it is being crucified. Remember: Whenever you give something up, it must be replaced with a filler. Whenever the enemy is cast out, he will come back to see if his old home is vacant. So let God fill you. Living every day with the Counselor and Comforter (Holy Spirit) is so amazing.

The new normal awaits you, the Father awaits you, healing awaits you, purpose awaits you, and a life you have yet to experience awaits you.

This new normal will take some getting used too, but there is no place that's better to be. God says, "See I am doing a new thing, are you not aware?" (Isaiah 43:19). What God is doing in you is fresh and new, and it will require change. You might feel uncomfortable at first, but you'll appreciate it in the end. Yes, God is demanding all of you. He is demanding more of you. This is the process of developing a relationship with Him. He is restoring your soul and leading you into a life you've never known.

You may be new to this, but in this new normal. God is healing you of your father-wound. Whenever God wants to heal someone, He puts the person in the same situation that broke them. This is the process of God healing you from the role that hurt you with the person He can trust over you. You're wondering who God is, and how to approach Him, how to address Him. Good, those are the questions that begin the seek. On this seek, don't stop until you have found him. You will never fully know God and that is why we will spend the rest of our lives seeking him. He is the reward, he is who we are really after. It is really God that we all want and desire. You may be asking God, "What should I call you?" God is speaking back to you today, saying,

"Call me, 'Dad.' I love you. You are no longer an orphan; you are my son, my daughter. Welcome home. This is your new normal."

ABOUT THE AUTHOR

Te'Aire Griffin is the founder of Restore Man Amour Ministries, located in Charleston, SC. Te'Aire has been commissioned to minister hope to a broken and fatherless generation. Te'Aire's overall goal is to turn the hearts of fathers back to their children and the hearts of the children back unto their fathers; most importantly guide those she leads to turn their hearts back to God as Abba. Te'Aire is a dynamic speaker and she releases words that bring listeners to their mandate place to be activated and stirred to pursue God and have a deeper relationship with him. Te'Aire is a teacher, exhorter, encourager, preacher, Youtuber and now Author. She has spoken at conferences, church services, colleges; as well as special guest panelist. After looking for love in all the wrong places she has personally restored her love back unto her natural father and Heavenly Father and she wants to help you do the same. Te'Aire is a picture example of Daughter of the King and a daughter WELL LOVED.